Amazingly Deep Roots

KNOWING THE **WHY** BEHIND **WHAT** YOU BELIEVE

Melissa Schworer

Amazingly Deep Roots

Knowing the Why Behind What You Believe

All Scripture passages in this book are taken from the Authorized King James Version, any deviations are not intentional.

DayStar Publishing

PO Box 464 • Miamitown, Ohio 45041

Published by Daystar Publishing

Miamitown, OH 45041

www.daystarpublishing.org

Also available at www.truthandsong.com

This book is dedicated to my husband. He is the iron that sharpens iron. He is patient with my endless questionings and ponderings and always points me back to God's word.

CONTENTS

INTRODUCTION

To get the most out of this devotional, I would encourage you read it through in this manner:

1. Each day, look at the specific question or thought that will be touched upon. This will set a context for the Scripture for the day.
2. MOST IMPORTANT: Read through each Scripture passage and see what stands out in regard to that day's thought or question.
3. Go through my commentary on that day's teaching and glean from any evidence or insight I have gotten from science, history or every day examples.

As this devotional is essentially a Bible study on the major things you will need to know about your beliefs as you step out into independence, it is important that you see what God says about each topic before hearing my thoughts.

If you just read the commentary without the Scripture, or just read the Scripture without understanding the thought process behind it, it will seem like you are getting puzzle pieces without seeing the big picture.

If you read it as recommended you will be able to see it as a whole.

Enjoy!

Part One

Dating, Romance & The Bible

Hi there. The season of life between 15 and 25 years of age just seems to be where nothing is more exciting as finding someone with whom you may settle down and "begin your life."

Isn't that horrible, thinking that life doesn't begin until you know who you will marry or if you will marry? And very often people struggle with this time of not knowing and just wish that there would be an answer one way or the other.

If I could live that season over with again, I can't say that I would do it much differently. I like to know things. I like to plan. I don't like having to live each day in faith and reliance on God. I struggle living life to the fullest in the moment. I seem to forget that "real life" isn't "some day, but that "real life" is right now.

But one thing I know for certain is this, while I am living "right now" to the fullest, I like to know what God has to say about things. That way when an opportunity arises I can make a decision in the moment with confidence.

And confidence in God's word is something we all need during times of the unknown. That is what I hope you can find as we study a little bit about this season of dating, romance and the single years.

Week One / Day One: Dating? Courting? Anything goes?

Hebrews 13:4, Proverbs 16:9

It is difficult to look at dating in our modern societies and compare it with Scripture. Arranged marriages aren't the norm in America, and there are so many single young women hoping to be married.

Not only that, but the idea of dating standards has kind of been on a pendulum in the past hundred or so years.

My grandmother was married at fifteen to my grandfather who was twenty and they stayed married their whole lives despite their ups and downs.

My mother and father met each other in church. There was a lot of dating during high school and most everyone went to a public school, Christian or not. This was before the Christian school movement.

In my youth, I went to a Christian school, a Bible College and then went on to meet my husband on the internet. I had never even heard of courting, except for one couple who practiced it at my college.

Then suddenly, the Purity Movement began with the book "Why I Kissed Dating Goodbye" and it was as if courting was the way to go.

A generation has since passed and I now see so many girls in their late twenties still "waiting for their Isaac," and Joshua Harris, the author of the book, recanted his philosophy and no longer believes the Bible.

We need to question whether something is man's philosophy or if it is Scriptural before we jump on a bandwagon.

Week One / Day Two: It is better to marry than to burn

1 Corinthians 7:1-9, 34-35

To be honest, the Bible has very little to say about how people are to meet their spouses. It does speak of the father's role, but I will talk about that later.

Paul's opinion was that if you can keep your lusts and purity under control, than he personally wished that more people would serve God as a single person.

To be honest, the single person does seem to have greater opportunity to do so. It costs so much less to live as a single person than as a family and if that is your focus, you can keep your cost of living and responsibilities to a minimum and give much of your time to the Lord.

But if a person is struggling with purity and the burning within, then Paul recommends that that person get married rather than live in the perpetual battle that comes with that.

You are probably thinking, "Well, yeah! I want to get married, but how do I get the right guy to notice me?"

You have very few Biblical limitations in that regard. In fact, I think tomorrow's passage is pretty interesting concerning that.

Week One / Day Three: The daughters of Zelophehad

Numbers 27:1-7, Numbers 36:1-7

I think this passage is fascinating, because it is so different than how we think.

I mean, when was the last time in America at least that a girl's inheritance was the deciding factor as to who she would marry?

But God wanted things done a certain way during this time period and the daughters of Zelophehad in today's passage were wise to seek counsel of God when something was questionable.

But what I think we can draw from this is consistent with the New Testament church age and that is how God said, "Let them marry to whom they think best." But it was within a specific perimeter.

For them, it had to be within the tribe of their fathers.

For us God gave us the boundary of "not being unequally yoked with unbelievers." 2 Corinthians 6:14

But this passage sets the precedent that when a father was unable to have a say in the situation, the girls were able to choose on their own within God's boundaries.

Week One / Day Four: Ruth

Ruth 3:6-18

Honestly, it would be better if you read the whole book of Ruth to get the big picture. But I couldn't help but notice some things that could be examined and might be applicable today.

1. I think it is interesting that Ruth didn't just sit at home worrying about what to do. (Ruth 2:1-2) She looked at her options and went to the place that had the best chances for meeting her needs.
2. I can't help but notice that her reputation was extremely important when Boaz noticed her. (Ruth 2:11)
3. It was obvious that Boaz paid Ruth special attention and favor and yet nothing was progressing. How many girls have been in that situation and seemed at a loss?
4. Naomi encouraged Ruth to discreetly make her intentions known to this man who was showing her favor. If we were in that situation, how could we discreetly do that in our culture?
5. Boaz was an older man. Now, I am not saying that it is wise for an 18 year old to start looking at 30 year old men as prime prospects, but as you mature, I want to encourage you in this principle: it is not "settling" if your expectations are Biblical (not cultural).
6. So many girls will compromise where God draws the line and yet draw so many lines that God has never drawn. (i.e. Choosing looks over a guy's spiritual condition.) Are you setting your expectations where God did not put them?
7. Boaz was kind of shy and seemed to feel "unworthy" of Ruth's attention. (Ruth 3:10)

Maybe the "nice guy" would make the best husband after all.

Week One / Day Five: Finding "Mr. Wrong"

2 Cor. 11:2, 1 Cor. 7:36-38, 1 Tim. 4:3, 1 Cor. 10:31, 2 Cor. 6:14, Matt. 5:32

In an age where divorce rates have more then doubled over the past century, it is good to be careful about who you marry. We are all concerned about marrying "Mr. Wrong."

Let me give you some biblical guidelines on how to not marry "Mr. Wrong."

1. If you have a wise and discerning father who raised you for the Lord and is invested in your life, than please, I beg of you, don't get involved with a guy without seeking his advice. Not only should you seek his advice, but you should very likely yield to it. I don't care how old you are, that principle is true.
2. Be not unequally yoked with an unbeliever. And to be honest, the more likeminded you are with your husband the easier your marriage will be in general. But as a Christian, marrying an unbeliever is a sin.
3. If a man has been divorced (save for the cause of fornication), you would be an adulterer to marry him. Statistically though, those who have been divorced[1] are more likely to get divorced. Keep that in mind.
4. Set biblical boundaries for purity and "Mr. Wrong" will very often reveal himself during the dating period one way or another.

The rest about a man is just personal preference, but we would be wise to choose one with godly characteristics. I talk about those later in the week on "Qualities of a good man."

---

1 https://www.wf-lawyers.com/divorce-statistics-and-facts/

Week One / Day Six: Youthful lusts

1 Corinthians 7:1, Proverbs 7:8, 2 Tim. 2:22, James 4:17

There are very few temptations in the world like the physical drive God put in us that He reserved for marriage.

My husband says that Satan tries everything he can do to get a young couple into bed before marriage and everything he can do to keep the married couple out of it.

But just as Daniel determined within himself not to defile himself with the king's meat, we have to set some boundaries as to how to keep ourselves from being defiled from our own lusts.

Paul tells us in 1 Cor. 7:1 that it is good for a man not to touch a woman, and in James 4:17 we see that "to him that knoweth to do good and doeth it not, to him it is sin." The Christian should abstain from physical touch with the opposite sex until marriage.

In Proverbs 7:8 we see how it was that the simple man fell to the power of the strange woman. He went near the corner of her street.

What Solomon is trying to tell us is to stay as far away from temptation as possible. "Yea, many strong men have been slain by her." (Prov. 7:26)

I try to tell every girl this one piece of advice, "Never, never, never be alone with a guy."

Week One / Day Seven: A good name

1 Thess. 5:22, 1 Cor. 15:33, Prov. 22:1, Ecc. 7:1

Never being alone with a guy and never being touched by a guy before marriage seems a little extreme, but I will tell you this, if you follow those principles, you will never find yourself having fallen to temptation.

You will also have your reputation intact and be honored as wise.

You will be obeying the principle of avoiding all appearance of evil.

And, you will be far less likely to be taken advantage of by a froward man.

But the opposite is also true. If you do not heed God's word of fleeing youthful lusts, avoiding the appearance of evil, making way for temptation like the simple man, and have a relationship where touching is okay, you will find yourself as many other girls who live with regret and shame for the rest of their lives.

I encourage Biblical living because it works. It is the best way.

But there are many temptations in regards to the burning lusts of the flesh before and after marriage. Of those, God says, "From such turn away." (2 Timothy 3:1-6) I want to cover more about them next week.

Week Two / Day One: Same sex attraction

Romans 1:24-28

I would be naive to think that just because you are reading this devotional that you have not had to face temptation.

Maybe your temptation is that you are attracted to someone of your own gender.

But honestly, is one sinful attraction very much different from another sinful attraction? For instance:

1. What if you were exposed to inappropriate pictures as a child and have developed a taste for or addiction to those images?
2. What if you started reading romance novels (Christian or not) and it stirred up lusts and fantasies within you that cause you to burn within, but you long to read them anyway. You love the way they make you feel?
3. What if you were abused as a child and now your lusts include abusive tendencies?
4. What if you have developed lustful, habitual secret sins?

It matters not our sin, but what matters is that we understand if it is a sin and how we respond to God's word.

Because if we do not understand God's opinion on a matter, we can be easily deceived, discouraged and trapped.

Next week I want to talk about just those things, what God has to say about lust, fornication, adultery and vile affections.

Week Two / Day Two: Same sex attraction

Romans 1:24-28, Leviticus 18

This topic was different for me growing up because a lot of my co-workers were homosexuals and nice people. And to be honest, I think if it hadn't been for the Bible, I would have had no problem with these types of relationships.

But you see, it *is* God who defines morality. Outside of God why would anything be labelled as "right" or "wrong?" Relativism would make perfect sense. I do what is right for me and you do what is right for you and as long as we choose to be respectful to each other, we are both "good."

I get it.

But we do have the Bible and if you believe that it is 100% trustworthy, than you need to accept it for what it says.

Today's passage very discreetly describes "vile affections." When you read the whole passage you can see that when it says, "Even women did change the natural use into that which is against nature. And likewise also the men, leaving the natural use of the woman, burned in their lust one toward another, men with men working that which is unseemly,"

This is consistent with God's view on the topic found in Leviticus 18:22. He said that man should not "lie with mankind, as with womankind: it is abomination."

So, for me, no matter my experiences in life, I knew that what God said was wrong was wrong and I needed to act accordingly.

Week Two / Day Three: The "burning of lusts" before marriage

1 Corinthians 7:1-9, Hebrews 13:4-5

There are so many questions that can be asked about physical relationships before marriage, but as I mentioned before, God is pretty clear that before marriage "It is good for a man not to touch a woman."

Still, there are other longings and desires that happen before marriage. And what if you remain single as an adult?

I was talking to a friend the other day who had a child in her teens and although her heart was to be married, she never met "Mr. Right" while she was raising her child.

I asked her thoughts on "the burning" and she said, "Stay away from things that would cause that within you." Like Hebrews 13:5 "be content with such things as ye have."

If you have a life of singleness, than bloom where you are planted. Don't read romance novels or watch sensual movies. Stay away from triggers that would cause your mind to wander.

Rather, be like the single person in 1 Corinthians 7 who spent their extra time serving the Lord with their whole heart.

But, if you consistently struggle even when all temptations are removed and avoided, then my suggestion is this - change things up in your life a bit and make preparation for marriage a priority.

Week Two / Day Four: The “burning of lusts” before marriage

1 Corinthians 7:1-9, 1 Corinthians 10:13

Now, I said yesterday, “Make preparation for marriage a priority.” Some of you might be thinking, “I *want* to get married. There just is nobody around to marry.”

But I believe that when you have earnestly tried to overcome a battle and are still fighting the fight daily against a besetting sin, that there *is* a way of escape. And strictly from a Biblical sense, Paul suggested marriage.

And I want to point back to last week where I said that we tend to draw lines where God hasn’t drawn them and then cross lines that God has placed.

This is one of those times where I would ask you to take a look at your situation and say, like I did before I got married, “Is there something I could do to better my odds of meeting someone?”

Maybe it’s:

- Being willing to move to another location.
- Attending a likeminded but larger church or Bible College somewhere else.
- Discerningly going on a dating site and limiting yourself to only likeminded believers.
- Working on your appearance and hygiene (taking better care of your hair, clothes, weight, skin, odor, teeth or makeup).
- Getting outside of your comfort zone and talking to people or inviting groups over to your house, or
- Working in a ministry or a job where you interact more with people

Week Two / Day Five: The "burning of lusts" before marriage

James 5:16-17

Even though marriage is what Paul suggested, it is not the final solution. If your heart is not willing to do whatever it takes to win against the besetting sin, then those same sins can still keep you in their chains as bad habits can then follow you.

One huge help in gaining victory over a sin is to have accountability. But sometimes we are too ashamed to admit our faults to anyone.

But if you want victory, then you must be willing to put aside your pride.

Seek a parent or godly mentor that you may pray with about your struggle and seek solutions to limit opportunity and temptation.

If you feel like there is no one you can trust, I know that the ministry "Reformer's Unanimous" has a strict privacy policy and is especially helpful in overcoming addictions.

Week Two / Day Six: Immodesty and fornication

Matthew 5:27-28

This week is dedicated to what God has to say about fornication and I would be missing something if I did not mention the connection God makes to adultery and the need for us to keep ourselves dressed in a way that would not draw attention to sensual aspects of our body.

While each man has a responsibility to keep his heart diligently and to keep his eyes pure (Job 31:1), God also counts us guilty for our part in the matter.

The Bible speaks of sensual areas. (Prov 5:19-21, Exodus 28:42, Isaiah 47:2-3)

I would encourage you to not only keep those areas covered, but also not to draw attention to them by wearing clothes that reveal every bit of your figure.

Webster's 1828 dictionary defines discreet as: prudent, wise in avoiding errors of evil, and in selecting the best means to accomplish a purpose, circumspect, cautious, wary, not rash.

Circumspect is an attitude of being aware of what is going on around you in case of danger. Cautious and wary have a similar feeling.

When in doubt, don't.

Week Two / Day Seven: Dating an unbeliever

2 Corinthians 6:14

The last thought on the topic of sins when it comes to romance and relationships is the one of dating and marrying unbelievers.

The Bible is pretty clear that we have no place marrying an unbeliever. It would make sense that if we wouldn't marry an unsaved guy we wouldn't date one either. Unfortunately, I didn't have that kind of sense when I was dating.

I used to "date guys for fun" but would not "seriously date" anyone who wasn't saved. Sure, I would witness to them. But to be honest, while they might have gotten saved or made a profession of faith, none of them are in church today.

I ended up missing out on good opportunities because of the bad opportunities I was taking. Their bad choices started rubbing off on me and I compromised in many of my beliefs.

Rather than casting your pearls before the swine (Matt. 7:6), stop looking at the pigpen at all and broaden your vantage point. There are far more good guys out there than you know.

Week Three / Day One: Qualities of a good man

Psalm 119

I have been married 16 years today. Since I have been married, I have seen many young couples divorce and some older couples as well.

I am going to give you my observations and some Scripture that I believe will point you to qualities in a spouse that will help save you from heartache, and will also help you to have a pleasant marriage.

The #1 thing that will help you to have a good marriage is if your husband loves the Bible more than he loves himself. As I read Psalm 119, I can't help but notice how much David (although not perfect) loved God's word.

God said he was "a man after God's own heart." I can't help but think that it has a little bit to do with how he sought after the Lord and truly relied upon the laws, precepts and scriptures that had been revealed.

When conflict arises or direction is needed, where does a godly man go? We have a saying in our home "He who has the most Scripture wins." Now, we really don't have much conflict because of this exact thing. We have unity because we unite under God's word.

A good man allows the Bible to be his final authority.

Week Three / Day Two: Qualities of a good man

Psalm 51

Yesterday I pointed out that whoever you marry should love God's word more than himself. One of the practical reasons for this is because God is the head of your husband and if he is not in the Bible, it is nigh impossible for him to be "led." The Holy Spirit speaks through God's word.

But a second reason is what you can see here in Psalm 51. David was a man with a tender heart towards repentance. When he was confronted with his sin, he did not respond like many of the kings in the Old Testament and "kill the prophet."

He submitted to the word of God (in this case, revealed by Nathan.)

I would encourage you to see how a guy responds when someone chastises him. Does he become easily angry? Does he "kill the messenger?" I guess, I am asking, does he respond as a scorner and fool or does he humbly seek truth from the Bible and repent if needed?

A good man responds well to correction.

Week Three / Day Three: Qualities of a good man

James 1:19-20, Prov. 22:24-25, Proverbs 16:32

It has been said that psychopaths can hide their tendencies for up to a year, but not much longer. Just keep that in mind as you start becoming serious about marriage.

It hurts my heart to hear stories of wives who say that their "husband seemed so nice until they got married."

The sad truth is that it is our responsibility to get to know someone well before we say "I do," but so many girls don't stop and ask the guy's friends and family how the person responds in anger.

But don't stop there. Ask how they deal with hurts. Do they tend to get bitter, sullen, moody or withdrawn? Or do they try their best to forgive and work through problems?

Because it is you who will bear the brunt of their emotions.

A good man is slow to wrath and quick to forgive.

Week Three / Day Four: Qualities of a good man

Proverbs 13:10, Galatians 5:13-21, Romans 1:29-31

Some personalities are prone to make the tough decisions (but also lack empathy), be problem solvers (and problem finders) and born to pursue a cause (but might ignore you if you aren't their focus at the moment.)

The Holy Spirit can help mold these people to be great leaders. I think of the Apostle Paul (who wasn't married by the way). He had to pave a path to teach grace rather than the law and there was no small amount of resistance. God needs men who can bear the burden and the fight won't wear them down.

Paul had this tough disposition, but you can see that as he grew older he encouraged Titus and Timothy to "be gentle." (2 Timothy 2:24, Titus 3:2)

My point is that God has a plan for each person, but it takes a spouse with a lot of grace, forgiveness and understanding to be married to these "kingly" types of men.

While he is out trying to fix the world, he might find that you need more "fixing" than anyone else.

This is my word of caution, do they seem to relish a good debate? Do they enjoy pointing out people's flaws? Are they gossipy and always the hero of a story?

If so, you might want to wait a while and watch to see how they grow in grace. A good man is humble.

Week Three / Day Five: Qualities of a good man

Luke 1:17, Malachi 4:6

Some men might not want children. That is okay. But I would ask them why.

Is it a propensity towards selfishness and they don't "want the responsibility" or is it something deeper?

The question of raising children can help bring up many issues held deep inside. Maybe there was abuse in their past. Maybe they are fearful of their ability to raise a child. It could be that they were the oldest in a large family and are just tired of being around children.

The reasons are endless, but a good man will not despise children.

Take time to get their childhood history and viewpoints of raising and ministering to children.

A good man will have a tender heart toward children.

Week Three / Day Six: Qualities of a good man

Hebrews 10:25, Exodus 20:3

I cannot stress this point enough. Is the guy you are interested in attending church faithfully?

I am not asking if he attends church. I am asking if he attends church faithfully.

Because his first love needs to be God.

If he regularly misses church for work, school, studying, rest, and activities out of town, there is reason to doubt his walk with the Lord.

He might be a great guy with good standards and while church attendance doesn't solely mean he is "godly," it does point to his priorities.

If you want to marry a man who will spiritually lead your family, he needs to show fruit of being spiritually led himself and that doesn't happen with spotty church attendance. Time will prove this true.

A good man is faithful to church.

Week Three / Day Seven: Qualities of a good man

Luke 16:1-13

Another area to consider about a possible spouse is their financial situation.

While not every guy will have a house, car and a savings plan, it would be wise to see how he manages his finances.

Is he wasteful? Is he in debt? Is he a hard worker? Does he believe that the man should provide for the home?

How does he feel about you spending money? How do you feel about you spending money? Are you on the same page?

Money management is one of the greatest sources of contention in a home because it affects the male ego and the woman's security.

You probably already know that I have written [2]"Faith and Finance - Peace With or Without Prosperity." I would encourage you to read it and before you enter a lifetime commitment with anyone be diligent to know what God and your future spouse think about financial management.

A good man will strive to be a good steward.

---

2 Can be ordered through www.amazon.com or www.truthandsong.com

Week Four / Day One: Qualities of a good woman

Proverbs 31:23

It is my opinion that a woman can either make or destroy a man. I have seen good men torn down and crippled and argued with to the point that they no longer gave an opinion, “interfered” with raising their children and also spent a lot of time quietly doing chores and cooking dinner for their “Christian” wife.

I have seen men compromise all they believed to get away from a contentious woman. Some even live the rest of their days happily married to another women, but they stayed out of church and their children wandered as well.

I have also seen a man with no presumed talents or gifts excel far beyond others' expectations. Not because he was pushed by his wife, but because she was a cheerleader and supported him at each turn.

A good woman is an asset whether single or married, and good women share some basic qualities. That is what we will talk about this week.

A good woman understands the impact she can make: for good or evil.

Week Four / Day Two: Qualities of a good woman

1 Peter 3:3-5

I will talk later a great deal about our relationship to authority and that area of trusting God. But I cannot emphasize enough that we can only truly have meekness and a quiet spirit when we put our trust in God. Let me talk a little bit more about trusting God in relation to marriage.

It is a great temptation to try to evoke change in other people with whom we disagree, but as I tell my daughters, "There are two things that will keep our temper and countenance in check. The first is when we realize that we can't control others. The second is when we learn to pray." But the third element of trusting the Lord is being long-suffering and patient.

Very often we want to see God work right now. We want answers. We want comfort. We want people to understand us. We want people to see things how we see them. And this transfers over to our relationship in marriage.

We want him to be a saver, or maybe be a little looser with how he views our spending. We want him to be more firm with children or a little less critical. We want him to be a better provider or to spend more time at home.

But what if God doesn't view your priorities as highly as you do? Are you willing to pray for God's will and let it rest in Him?

A good woman trusts God.

Week Four / Day Three: Qualities of a good woman

Titus 2:4, Prov. 23:31-35, Prov. 20, 1 Timothy 3:11

I have always been a little bit of an old soul, but I can also be very silly and I also forget how many times the Bible says that women are to be sober.

There are two definitions for sober and I think we should be both. The first pertains to alcohol. The Bible speaks throughout Scripture of the dangers of wine and strong drink and to stay away from it.

The second definition is with respect to having a serious mindset. I think this has to do with the fear of the Lord. We should live our lives in light of the judgment of God, knowing that we will give an account of our lives.

So many mistakes are made simply because we don't seriously consider the impact of our choices on the lives of those around us.

Taking seriously what God has to say about things is important, because it literally is part of being "sober minded."

A good woman is serious about her choices, not flippant.

Week Four / Day Four: Qualities of a good woman

Proverbs 31:26, James 3:13-18

How many times does the Bible talk about a tale bearer, a false accuser, a meddler, one who causes strife and contention, or speaks without gentleness?

And yet, isn't it easy to be snippy, argumentative or speak your mind without grace because they "need to hear the truth?"

But my pastor says, "It only takes one bomb to go off for the damage to be done."

It takes a long time to restore your reputation if you develop one of being rash, emotional, sharp-tongued or a false accuser.

I have a friend who made the choice as a teen that she never wanted to be the girl about whom someone said, "Did you hear what she said about …?" She believed that if she never spoke ill or gossipy about someone but rather was an encourager and kind, then she would not have those moments of regrets.

It did not mean that she never had to confront someone, but she did it privately and with grace.

A good woman speaks with kindness, gentleness and grace.

Week Four / Day Five: Qualities of a good woman

Proverbs 11:22, Titus 2:5

When I was a child, my father regularly said, “Melissa. Discretion.”

And to be honest, I literally had no idea what discretion even meant.

I just felt like I should be me and to be anything else was a hypocrite. This led to quite a few awkward conversations throughout life. I just said whatever I felt and believed, regardless of the crowd.

But several years ago, I prayed that God would give me discretion of my mouth and what an embarrassing few years followed. I feel like every mistake I could have made I made, and in public nonetheless.

I was pulled aside by a good friend who said, “You make people feel uncomfortable when you talk about that.” Now, this wasn’t the first time I had heard that, but it was the first time I took it to heart.

But discretion has to do with being circumspect and being aware of what is going on around us. I think of the soldiers who fought with Gideon. 1) They stayed upright and cautious as they drank water from their hands. 2) They were on guard. 3) They were careful. 4) They didn’t take unnecessary risks and 5) They had discernment and knew how to best carry themselves.

Discretion can be applied to our mouths, to our clothes and to our choices.

A good woman chooses to be cautious, guarded and careful of her surroundings and how her actions can hurt or help others.

Week Four / Day Six: Qualities of a good woman

Proverbs 9:6-11

One of the qualities that for me was a top priority in a husband was a man who could tell me “No!” without causing me to want to fight or defend myself. I remember the first time my husband gently said, “Melissa, you need to stop talking right now.” It was a tough pill to swallow.

Then just yesterday, I was trying to explain why I felt that a project I was working on wasn’t as good as I wanted it to be, but he said he felt it was great. Well, I kept trying to prove my point and he said, “Melissa, you can out talk me any day but the only result is that I will stop giving you my opinion.” You see how nicely he corrected me?

But if I got offended every time I was rebuked I would lose such valuable insight and opportunities to grow.

I used to be so defensive until I understood that there is truth to be gained in even the accusations of an “enemy” (also, often known as anyone who disagrees with us) and growing in truth and understanding is worth it.

I still do get my feelings hurt because I tend to be a people pleaser, but I have learned to just correct my actions if the admonitions are Biblical and quietly hope the change will be seen in me over time. This feels weird to be talking solely about me, because then it seems as if I am praising myself. But more importantly, I don’t want you to make the same mistakes I did.

A good woman will take reproof and appreciate the rebuker for speaking the truth … even if it wasn’t done “in love.”

Week Four / Day Seven: Qualities of a good woman

Philippians 2:3, Ephesians 5:21, 1 Corinthians 6:1-7, Matthew 5:40, 41

A principle I try to teach over and over to my daughters is that of esteeming others better than ourselves and to have a "Sure, no big deal" attitude when it comes to sharing or not getting our own way.

It is much easier said than done, and I want to be clear about something. This is not done as a form of weakness and out of fear that someone will be mad at us if we don't give them their own way. I am not encouraging you to be a doormat.

What I am saying is just the opposite. What I am suggesting takes great strength of mind, power and meekness.

It is purposely finding a way to have peace, understanding and be mutually beneficial. It is the heart of a servant who seeks the good of others in the service of God.

There is so much to be said about the servant who serves God with singleness of heart and not to be seen of men, but just because they know it pleases the Lord.

Whether it is in service to your husband, church, ministry, employer or home, it is choosing to serve the Lord rather than adopting the heart of the martyr that makes the biggest difference in a woman.

A good woman serves humbly.

Part Two

Day-to-Day Relationships

In this next section I try to focus on the most important relationships you will have and how to deal with the inevitable conflicts that will arise.

It is how we live the day-to-day that causes our light to shine brightly.

But if we don't invest in others or if we burn bridges without just cause we will find life to be rather lonesome in our time of need and in times when we might have been just what someone else needed.

What is life if it is lived and died in one's own needs without reaching out to others?

Still, life can become lonely at any stage. As exciting as it is to meet that special someone, a large portion of your time probably won't be spent with them. We sleep for 8 - 9 hours, and a husband's job can take up to 10 or more hours a day with lunch and commuting time.

Farther into adulthood, our high school and college friends are often also occupied in their new lives and responsibilities.

That is why it is important to make our day-to-day relationships a priority, and our first priority needs to be time with our best Friend: God.

Week Five / Day One: What does God want from our relationship with Him?

Philippians. 2:13, Rev. 4:11, Psalm 147:11

Without a doubt, our relationship to God is the most important one that there is. If we don't understand Him and who He wants to be to us or who He wants us to be to Him, we could honestly waste our lives.

I think about that quote by D.L. Moody, "Our greatest fear should not be of failure, but of succeeding at something that doesn't really matter."

Because what really is the purpose of your existence? Why did God put people here if He knew they would fail Him? Why did He give them free will? Does He actually have a specific plan for your life?

There was a purpose for each person before Christ ever died and before the Great Commission. Each person and each creation was here for God's pleasure.

But God sincerely enjoys His creation when they are walking in His will.

So, I guess the question naturally arises, "What is God's will for our lives?"

Week Five / Day Two: What is God's will for our lives? Thankfulness

1 Thess. 5:18

Someone said many years ago, "Rather than searching for the 'big things' in our lives, we should rather practice the everyday things that we already know are God's will."

Because honestly, to "brighten the corner where you are" doesn't mean we are going to be gigantic lighthouses. In fact, many people are candles, flashlights and lanterns. We reach the people in our part of the world, or city or town.

If you look at Jesus's life, He basically traveled within the same small areas of Israel throughout His life. He obeyed God's will for His life and let God handle the results.

With that in mind, I want to focus on the verses that speak of God's will and what we can learn from them and how they will help us please God.

Today's verse is simple in nature, but harder in practice.

It is God's will that we be thankful: no matter our circumstance. The first step to a bitter heart is when we forget to be thankful.

Week Five / Day Three: What is God's will for our lives? Abstaining from fornication

1 Thess. 4:3, 2 Tim. 2:22

Out of all of the things that God could say are His will for our lives, He put this in His word.

I have said it many times before, but the way you stay out of fornication is not by being strong in the midst of it. It is by fleeing the temptation.

Don't be alone with a guy.

There are plenty of things you can say to each other to get to know each other on the phone without having to spend hours alone in temptation's way.

It is also good to have a plan on your phone where you have an accountability partner who can review texts and usage. There is hope for purity if you are humble enough to seek help and abstain even from the appearance of evil.

Week Five / Day Four: What is God's will for our lives? Be not conformed to the world

Romans 12:2, 2 Cor. 6:17, Titus 2:14

I have seen grown adults with children do an about face in what they believe and practice because they did not obey Romans 12:2.

There aren't a lot of gray areas in the Bible, but in relation to culture and conforming to the world it seems to get a little sticky.

My kids have asked me questions about blue, purple, pink, red, etc. hair, nose rings, ear rings all the way up the ear, ear gauges and fake tattoos. Why are they considered wrong if the Bible doesn't specifically say so?

Honestly, this is a heart issue, because God does have these verses about being distinctly different from the world and yet teaches also to be modest (in this case I refer to propriety and to not being inappropriate culturally).

But as one who loves to study history and cultures, I know that the farther a people or civilization has gotten from God, the more they distort their natural appearance. As you look at pagan history, you will see that our culture is literally going backwards.

My philosophy is that Satan hates that man was made after the image of God and although we do not look exactly like Him (due to the fall), we resemble Him enough that Satan keeps trying to mutilate us.

Either way, my personal view is, "When in doubt, don't."

Week Five / Day Five: What is God's will for our lives? Transformed by the renewing of your minds

Romans 12:2, Romans 16:18

My father used to tell me the story of how when bankers were being trained to recognize fake money, they were never actually shown fake money. They just dealt with real money so much that the fake seemed obvious.

And yet we live in a time where God said many will be deceived by none other than "good words and fair speeches."

I have watched this happen and it is because these "false teachers" look so much like they are speaking the truth. They say half of truth and leave the other half out.

For instance, no one will argue with this statement. "Pure religion and undefiled before God and the Father is this, To visit the fatherless and widows in their affliction."

But to leave out the rest of the verse would lead someone to believe that "good works" are all that it takes to please the Lord and we should become community leaders.

But the rest of the verse says, "and to keep himself unspotted from the world."

How easily we can be deceived if we are not renewing our minds in the Bible enough to know when we are being deceived through partial truths. A counterfeit looks almost exactly like the real thing.

Week Five / Day Six: What is God's will for our lives? Keep His commandments

John 14:15, John 15:10, Romans 5:1, 2 Tim. 2:15

Following the same train of thought from yesterday, we have many well-meaning "Christ followers" who, as best as they know how, "love Jesus."

They don't want to be caught up in the entrapments of empty religion.

Boy, do I agree with not getting caught up in the entrapments of empty religion.

Because we do not need "religion" to be accepted into heaven. We need the blood of Christ alone.

But to be a "Christ follower" or to "love Jesus" indeed goes beyond salvation. It has to do with growing "in Christ" and obeying His commandments.

There is so much more in the Bible beyond the gospel but I still want to talk a little bit more about the gospel and being "in Christ."

Week Five / Day Seven: What is God's will for our life? To be "In Christ"

Romans 3:24, Romans 8:1-2, 38-39, Eph. 1:13 & 4:30

There is a lot of doctrinal meat surrounding the term "in Christ" but it has everything to do with the gospel for the New Testament Christian.

The world existed about 4000 years before the term "in Christ" was even mentioned in the Bible. We are a special people in a special time period.

We do not have to follow the Old Testament laws. We do not need a human high priest, because Christ fulfilled the law and stands in our place. Indeed our redemption is literally found "in Christ."

Therefore to receive redemption we must get "in Christ." This seems pretty basic for those who grew up in a Christian home, but it is something that a lot of people don't understand.

Something happens when we accept Christ's gift of salvation and the blood atonement for our sins. We are placed inside the spiritual Body of Christ, held tight by the hands of God and sealed by the Holy Spirit until the day of redemption.

In Christ, we are safe and eternally secure. But being in Christ is far more than the basic understanding of salvation

Week Six / Day One: Who are we "In Christ?"

2 Cor. 5:17, Rom. 5:8-10, 1 John 3:10, Isa 64:6

God saved us in spite of our sin. We were His enemies and we were children of Satan. But He also knew that we had no power over sin on our own and that our righteousness was nothing more than filthy rags.

But then ...

... we were born again.

And so, in Christ, we are no longer who we once were.

We have the opportunity to please God and do good and break free from the chains of our past. He no longer sees your sins, but the blood of Christ.

We are new creatures with a specific purpose and at this point we can move and grow beyond living for ourselves or living to please others.

We can sincerely live to please God. But as I mentioned before, pleasing God includes keeping His commandments and part of His commandments are not just doing good but abstaining from evil.

Week Six / Day Two: We have power over sin "in Christ."

Romans 6:1-6, Gal. 3:26 - 29

In today's passage you see the term (vs. 3) "baptized into Jesus Christ" and this is a spiritual baptism. (Did you know there are seven baptisms?) I just mentioned that because I did not want you to think that you had no power over sin until you were baptized at church.

This baptism in Romans 6 happens at the moment of salvation and it is when our old spirit dies and our new spirit is born again "in Christ."

So many times I hear Christian's saying, "Well Christ died for the sinner. He loved the sinner. Therefore, Christ loves me in my sin. He accepts me as I am: a sinner. He loves me just as much as a sinner as He does when I am living righteously."

In fact, I even heard a preacher on a well-known Christian program say, "And I pleaded with God that He would take away this besetting sin from my life, and I heard God's voice within me say, 'It was for that sin I died.' At that moment I knew that it was okay that this sin would never leave me."

Well, that is a deception wrapped up in truth. It is almost as if the sin has value because Christ died for it. The words are all true, but the conclusion is false.

The truth is that God hates sin, and in Christ we are freed from its power. "Shall we continue in sin that grace may abound? God forbid."

Week Six / Day Three: We are children of God "in Christ."

Romans 8:1-17, 2 Cor. 1:21-22, Gal. 3:26 - 29

Today has a lot of reading. That's okay, right? The average person can read one page of the Bible in 3 minutes. So, 17 verses isn't really a lot.

What I want to point out is that in Romans 8:1 you see that the whole context is about someone who is in Christ and as it moves through the passage it says that those who are in Christ have the Spirit of God and Christ in them.

This is where we get the term "ask Jesus into your heart."

But it also says that if Christ is in us then we are adopted into God's family and are His children and heirs with Christ.

This is important, because for God to kick us out of His family (or for us to lose our salvation), God would have to break a contract with Christ and His inheritance. You see, we are joint-heirs *with* Christ. If we don't get the inheritance, neither does Jesus and that just isn't going to happen.

So, not only are we in Christ, in God's hands and sealed by the Holy Spirit but we are also in a binding contract with God. We receive a lot at the moment of salvation.

That is a lot of technical information that matters quite a bit, but I want to talk about what being a child of God means to you right now.

Week Six / Day Four: We are a work in progress "in Christ."

Romans 8:18-30, Ephesians 1:4

The first thing that Paul talks about in these verses is that we have hope and help in troubles and purpose for our trials.

Not only that, but we also have the Holy Spirit who prays for us when the pains are so deep that there are no words to express them.

We have a God who can orchestrate even the worst of situations to bring glory to His name if we will trust Him and love Him.

SIDE NOTE: As you read further in the passage, you will notice the words "foreknow" and "predestinate." I want you to take note that this entire chapter first started with describing that this passage is written to those who are "in Christ" and in Ephesians 1:4 it says that we are chosen "in him."

This was something that was confusing to me when I was a late teen. Was I already predestined to salvation? But if you look at the context, what it is saying is that that God "foreknew" who would choose Christ and according to both Eph. 1:4 and Romans 8:29-30 what He predestined was this ...

Those who are "in Christ" are predestined to be holy, without blame and conformed to the image of Christ.

And so, all those sufferings and trials can be used to make us more like Christ, who also through sufferings learned obedience. (Heb. 5:8)

Week Six / Day Five: We have a family and place in heaven "in Christ."

Galatians 3:28, Ephesians 2:6, 11- 19, Colossians 3:10-11

As I look back through these past couple of days of devotions I can't help but think about how the afflictions of the righteous are many, but as David said, "I have not seen the righteous forsaken."

One of the wonderful things about being secure in Christ is that we literally have a place in heaven right now and we have each other. In Christ, it doesn't matter what nationality or genealogy or pedigree you have. We are all one and we are all connected in that way that only God can do.

He broke down the partition between Jew and Gentile as He broke down the wall between God and the sinner and we were drawn near to each other and near to God "in Christ." Never do we have to be alone.

While some have no mother, father, sister or brother on earth, in Christ we have a whole new family.

And as we sit in Christ at the right hand of the Father, we have access in prayer any time and any place.

This reminds me of the hymn, "No, never alone. No, never alone. He promised never to leave me, never to leave me alone." We can rejoice in that today.

Week Six / Day Six: We have faith, love and victory in Christ

1 Timothy 1:12-14, 2 Timothy 3:15, 1 John 5:1-5

I love this passage in 1 Timothy where Paul shares his testimony of how he had done so many things but in Christ he found faith and love.

I also can't help but notice how faith and love and the commandments of God are tied together in 1 John 5.

Do you remember how we talked about being children of God and having a family in Christ? Yet, John acknowledges that it is still a choice to love our family. Stranger yet is the best way he gives for us to actually love one another. He didn't give us a feeling or a list of good works. He said that we best love each other when we keep God's commandments.

As I pondered that, I thought how true that is because God's commandments are, like John said, "not grievous." They actually help us to be better people in many different ways.

Can you think of some commandments that help us to have better relationships with people? I will explore those further later on, but I just want to touch on "faith" before we go any further.

Week Six / Day Seven: We have faith, love and victory in Christ

Ephesians 6:11-18, Proverbs 3:5-6

If you have watched any of my videos on Youtube[3], you will know that I talk quite a bit about our shield of faith.

It is one thing to have faith in the blood of Christ or faith in the gospel, but as we grow and become more like Christ we start to learn the promises of God and how they impact us day to day.

For instance, one of my favorite promises is that He will lead us if we simply seek His will and trust His word (and lean not on our own understanding.)

It can be scary making decisions about the future, but we can have peace as we wait upon His direction and leading.

But can we truly trust God? Is it stupid to put faith in words in a book?

3www.youtube.com/c/melissaschworer

Week Seven / Day One: Faith in God

Luke 17:1-5

You know the age-old question, "How can God be good and still let bad things happen to good people?"

That is a legitimate question.

I remember when my husband's dad died, he wondered something similar. His dad was a good guy and young and yet he died of cancer before he ever saw his first grandchild.

I think of a family whose son died overseas from an IED (improvised explosive device). He was a good guy.

I think of another family who lost their son to suicide. He just struggled with the day-to-day battle of the mind.

Then there are countless victims of abuse, floods, earthquakes and war. Why doesn't God intervene?

I remember wondering this when my parents got divorced.

This is a type of faith that has to go beyond "the easy answer." But I will show from Scripture how God is just, good and merciful and why people suffer.

Week Seven / Day Two: Understanding God is Just

Hebrews 5:8, 11:37, 2 Tim. 3:12 Psalm 119:67-75, Psalm 107:17, Psalm 82:1-8, Matt. 24:3-14, Titus 1:2, Romans 3:3-6

There are many reasons that people suffer. They all are related to sin.

- God allows free will. People can choose to obey God or to disobey Him. He simply will not force people to obey and when people sin they hurt other people. David addresses this seeming injustice in Psalm 82 and his conclusion is resting in God's longsuffering and the day of judgment.

- God at times afflicts us or allows affliction and suffering to teach us to obey and *keep us from sin.* Jesus learned obedience through the things He suffered. Are we better than Christ? Therefore God will allow suffering in our lives to cause us to be more like Christ.

- David described it well when he said that before he had been afflicted he had gone astray and it was good that he was afflicted. Sometimes earthquakes, wars and floods are a judgment.

- 2 Timothy 3:12 and Hebrews 11:37 and countless other Scriptures show the persecution of those who live godly and righteous lives for Christ. In this world we will have tribulation, because the god of this world hates God and hates His children. And yet, God says of the martyrs that they are those of whom the world was not worthy. They will receive their just reward for their sacrifice.

Well, I am out of room. I guess we will cover more tomorrow.

Week Seven / Day Three: Understanding God is Just

Job 1:12, 19, Romans 5:12, Gen. 3:17-20

- We see from the story of Job that Satan wants to tempt us to sin and to curse God. Sometimes, God allows bad things to happen to good people for His own glory and to test and try His own people. Sin is in our nature and when bad things happen (whether from God or from Satan), we have an opportunity to simply trust God.

- Lastly, although I am sure there might be more I overlooked, suffering happens because of sin. Sometimes people die and get sick just because our bodies and earth are cursed. It isn't a judgment or a chastisement. It is just part of death that came from the garden of Eden. But someday, it will all be made new. What a day, glorious day, that will be!

Honestly though, God's ways are so beyond our ways. Because the next logical question is, "If sin brings all this suffering, than why did God allow sin in the first place?"

Week Seven / Day Four: Understanding God is Just

Jeremiah 29:13, Psalm 105:4, Psalm 27:8, 2 Chronicles 7:14

This goes back to the beginning of this whole section. God allowed sin because He wanted man to choose Him.

If you have ever played a game where you control every move and every action of the character, you can understand this a little better.

Man's free will and choice is part of us bringing pleasure to God.

There is such a difference between when someone spends time with you because it is required (like some school classes) versus when someone spends time with you because they enjoy you.

But along with the free will to choose God is the free will to choose evil and whether we agree or not, it was God's will to do it that way.

I personally am glad that I have the choice to pray or not to pray, because when I sit with Him, it is something I can give Him of myself. When I choose to do right despite my fleshly desire, He knows I did it for Him.

But I am glad that some day, all the wrongs will be judged and I am also thankful that my wrongs will be under the blood of Christ.

I want to start on a new thought tomorrow.

Week Seven / Day Five: Understanding God is just

Psalm 19:1-7, Romans 1:18-21

While trying to understand God, I am reminded of something my daughters asked me yesterday, "Mom. Do people who have never heard about God still go to hell? That is so sad."

It is good to trust that God's understanding is beyond our own and that He has revealed truth in His word. Today's verses (especially Romans 1:20) show that God deems all men without excuse.

I think about Prince Kaboo (a.k.a. Samuel Morris) and his testimony of God using an angel to release him from the stocks and lead him to a missionary. When someone is seeking light, and Christian's are obeying the Great Commission, God has consistently done amazing things to reveal His light to them.

An evangelist recently said, "If someone has never heard of God and therefore they automatically get pardoned from sin due to ignorance, we should never, ever share the gospel with anyone." But God is holy and sin cannot enter His presence and Jesus's blood is the only thing that can cover our sins.

This convicts me of our need to spread the gospel to every creature. Imagine if the missionary had NOT been in [4]Prince Kaboo's area. What a wonderful thing to be there right when someone needed the gospel.

As we are trying to understand God better, I hope this week has answered some questions.

4The Samuel Morris Story, The Torchlighters – Heroes of the Faith

Week Seven / Day Six: Understanding God is good

Matt. 19:17, Mark 10:18, Luke 18:19, Psalm 84:11, Ecc. 3:13, Ecc. 5:19

One thing that can be difficult to believe in the midst of suffering is that God is good or that God wants us to enjoy anything.

It is good to remember that this train of thought is a lie, "Christians can't do anything fun. They can't drink, do drugs, smoke, party or get involved physically with anyone until they are married … and who knows if they will ever get married. All they have left is eating." *(This has led to a lot of people justifying gluttony and a martyr mentality.)*

But God allows us so many things.

There are few things I enjoy more than playing the piano and singing harmony for the Lord.

But I think about horses, kittens and puppies, spending time with nieces and nephews and young children, serving in church ministry, leading someone to the Lord, hiking to the top of a mountain and seeing the valley below, watching spring flowers emerge after the winter, baking bread, a room after it is freshly painted, sunshine on my shoulders, quietly swimming laps, feeling the ocean pull the sand from beneath my feet, watching the sunset on the horizon, stormy skies with sunbeams peaking through, sailing on a quiet day, studying and mastering a topic and visiting with friends.

There is so much more, but I think you get the idea. God is not a scrooge. There is nothing good about working all week to drink away the weekend. Christians can experience so much more if they choose.

Week Seven / Day Seven: Understanding God is merciful

Psalm 136, 2 Samuel 12:15-23

I guess the longer I have been a Christian, the more I seem to appreciate the "for ever" part of God's mercy.

Not only does God forgive the sins of the youth, but He forgives the sins that we keep doing over and over and over.

I told my son, "You remind me a lot of King David. You are both gentle and masculine." He slyly replied, "You mean I remind you of a murderer?"

One thing about King David is that he was quick to repent. You don't see him justifying his sins or his actions.

And David knew that God was both merciful and gracious. I love how he says, "Who can tell whether God would be gracious to me?"

To understand God, we need to understand how even the vilest sinner can move the Lord to compassion (I think of Nineveh in the book of Jonah) when their heart is repentant.

Praise the Lord, for His mercy endureth forever.

Week Eight / Day One: Learning the importance of obedience to authority

1 Peter 3:4-6, Mark 11:27-33

If there was one thing to which I could accredit the relative "success" of my life, it would be that I was taught the Biblical viewpoint of authority.

If you are reeling that I even put "authority" in here, than I would gently urge you to question that gut reaction.

Now there will always be people who abuse authority, and it is true that very often "abusers" seek positions of authority so that they can keep their victims in a feeling of helplessness and subjection. But that is not the kind of authority I am talking about here.

What I am talking about is how important it is to understand that someone (not you) has the final say, and also equally important to your life is how you respond to that.

It is no secret that 1 Peter 3:4-6 are some of my favorite verses. I grew up in upstate New York and women there are bred to be feminist. I was no exception. I was raised in church my whole life, but it still took me a while to appreciate (yes, I literally mean appreciate and be thankful for) those in authority over me. It took even longer to understand this passage in 1 Peter.

But today I want you to think about how you truly feel about the idea that you are under someone's authority and that you may have to obey something even if you don't necessarily agree.

Week Eight / Day Two: This one is so hard

2 Timothy 2:1-14, 1 Cor. 14:34-35

Our relationship with those in authority is tricky. I remember the first time I read this passage, like *really* read it. It was awful. I did not notice where it said to pray for and be thankful for all men and especially kings and all that are in authority.

I especially didn't notice that it was Paul (who spent a lot of time in jail and still spoke with respect to Festus) who was writing it.

I am sure that I glazed over the part where it said, "That we may live a quiet and peaceable life."

I didn't think about the fact that this was good in God's sight (much like the meek and quiet spirit).

What stuck out to me most were the words "Let the women learn in silence will all subjection." Right?!?!

It took me until about the 7th year of marriage to really appreciate how God's wisdom was so beyond mine and how this issue of "the woman was deceived" was at the heart of it all.

But the thing is, even if I didn't understand *why* God said that, I had already learned the wisdom of obeying *before* I understood. "Lean not upon thine own understanding" is ringing in my head right now.

Week Eight / Day Three: Why are women under authority?

2 Tim. 3:1-6, Acts. 13:50, Job 2:9, Gen. 16:1-6

First of all, not everyone is your authority, but chances are that right now you are under the authority of your father, government and the general authority of your local church.

But it is the rare exception in the New Testament where you see a female without someone as her leader, guide or accountability. This is actually a good thing.

At the same time, women do *have* authority in different areas. We are to teach children and younger women. But our strengths of being sensitive to the leading of the Holy Spirit and highly aware of that "sixth sense" of feelings in general leave us weak to the deception of false spirits.

I have seen many females blatantly disobey God's word and say, "Well, I prayed about it and have peace. I just feel like the Holy Spirit isn't convicting me about this. So it must be okay."

There are plenty of good examples of women being key helpers in ministry, but we must not disregard the damage that can be done when women are deceived and pushing their own agenda.

I think of the phrase, "Women polish the bullets and give them to the men to fire." This means that when a woman gets upset she can rile up her husband and send him into a battle that God did not ordain.

Week Eight / Day Four: What is a good response to authority?

Hebrews 13:7, Romans 13:1-7, Prov. 29:1, 1 Peter 3:4-6

What's a girl to do? The very best thing you can do is to trust God and obey His word. This may mean that when you don't necessarily trust your husband's decisions that you can trust God to take care of you in spite of them.

I remember going to my pastor's wife and asking, "My husband wants me to support him in a decision, but I disagree with him 100%. How do I be respectful but let him know I disagree? I can't be excited about his idea like he is."

Do you know I handled it? *(Also, it is good to note that I literally cannot remember what it was about. But you bet if I had dug in my heels, it would have sent our marriage in the wrong direction and it would still be a point of contention.)*

I said something like, "I want you to know that I disagree with your decision and I just can't get excited about it like you are. But I love you. I trust God will bless our marriage if I follow you with a sweet spirit. I am sorry if I struggle with my spirit, but I will do whatever you say. I am struggling trusting you, but I trust God."

And do you know what? God is faithful. He is good. I truly have the best marriage. My husband is my best friend and he considers me *his* best friend.

Week Eight / Day Five: What is a good response to authority?

Hebrews 13:7, 1 Peter 2:13, 1 Pet. 5:5

The best thing you can do to learn to be a good wife or minister to God is to learn how to apply yesterday's principle of "trusting God and obeying His word even if you doubt your husband's decisions."

When I say "Trusting God" I very literally mean obeying His word. This can apply to every situation in life. If your parents mess up and make a bad decision: obey (unless they are asking you to sin).

It is so easy to become our own enemy when we are deceived by "righteous indignation."

It goes something like this, "My parents said that I could do this, but then they completely lied and didn't let me."

Were your parents wrong? Maybe. Is it right to have a bad attitude and go against their final wishes? Nope. God will honor you if you obey your authority.

Here is another one, "My youth pastor called out a kid in class and I just think how they did that was so wrong."

What if they were wrong? Is it okay to gossip and cause problems in the youth group? Nope.

To be honest, this is when the whole "women are to be silent in church" comes in really well.

Week Eight / Day Six: Does God even want you to obey the government?

Matthew 22:21, Romans 13:1-7, 2 Peter 2:10-19, 1 Timothy 2:1-3

I remember in college learning about speeding, disobeying copyright laws and other "acceptable Christian sins." The idea that speeding was wrong shocked me. "Why was it wrong?" I asked.

My teacher took the class to Romans 13 and explained that as Christians we are to obey our governments because they are of God.

The impact this discussion had upon me was life changing. It brought about the issue of "situational ethics." When was it okay to not obey your authority? Was it ever okay to speed? What about governments that are crooked and corrupt, what then?

The times where God allows disobedience are few and far between. You can find them in:

1) Acts 4:1-22 (esp. 19, 20) – The apostles preaching.
2) Daniel 6 – Daniel praying to God.
3) Exodus 1:17 – The midwives keeping the Israelite babies alive.

As a rule of thumb, God would have us to pray for our leaders and if the opportunity arises we can follow the example of Paul in Acts 26 where Paul respectfully approaches his leaders to plead his cause.

I take great comfort in remembering that Paul was alive during the violent rule of Nero and still he was peaceful to his leaders while still faithful to the gospel.

Week Eight / Day Seven: Why your heart attitude toward authority matters

Psalm 138:2, Proverbs 26:27

Are you still reading? I was just talking to my husband and telling him that this is such a hard topic to cover. I was afraid that you girls would stop the devotional and choke on the spiritual meat that I have been feeding you these past few weeks.

But I knew that I needed to swallow my fears and cover this topic anyway: for you.

Because I 100% believe that you cannot have a good relationship with God if you do not have this down.

I believe you cannot have a good relationship with your family, husband, employer or even your government if you have not learned how to have a sweet "sure, why not" attitude and obey regardless of how you feel.

If we sat down and talked I could give you so many examples of women who have become "survivors" of so much hurt, but it was hurt they brought upon themselves because they "did it their own way."

I am not being critical. I am trying to spare you the tremendous burdens that come when we "follow our heart" rather than follow our authority: God's word.

Week Nine / Day One: Friends

Proverbs 22:24, Proverbs 13:20

In my life friendships have ebbed and flowed. I moved around quite a bit before I was even seven, but when I was eight I lived in the same place until I was fifteen. During those years I met my childhood best friend who ended up marrying my brother.

Then when I moved as a teen I ended up in a small rural town with no one my age in my church and my brother and sister having moved out in previous years. And you know what? It turned out to be a blessing. I was able to spend some extra time with my parents, but it wasn't without loneliness.

Then as I moved away to Bible college, I had more friends than I could keep up with and made memories and bonds that have remained until this day.

But as marriage became my next season of life, loneliness reared its ugly head again. It's hard to believe that you can be married and lonely, but a husband isn't the same as female friends. But marriage changes things and Paul is right, a married woman cares for the things of the world and how she may please her husband. Now with five children, and my writing, making time for friends looks like two to three get-togethers a year.

My point is this: friends come and friends go. So, don't compromise for friends. Chances are that they won't even be around when you are reaping the consequences.

Week Nine / Day Two: Friends

Galatians 6:1, Proverbs 22:9, 19, 23

Friends are so wonderful. Well, wise friends are wonderful. But today I want to talk about how to be the friend that God wants you to be.

The first is to know when to speak up and when to keep your mouth shut.

Have you ever heard the phrases, "Familiarity breeds contempt," or "We always hurt the ones we love"? They are true because when we hang around someone a lot, we know the good and the bad about them and they can really start to get on our nerves.

They might do things that are different than how we would do them. They might have standards that are different from ours. They might chew loudly, and nobody should have to endure that!

What's a girl to do?

The first thing I want to ask you is this: is what they are doing clearly a sin? The second thing I want to ask you is: are they overtaken in it?

If the answer to both of these is "No" than I would recommend that you keep your mouth shut. This is a time for you to abide in the spirit and practice some temperance, meekness and longsuffering.

Week Nine / Day Three: Friends

Matthew 7:1-6, 18:15-17, James 3:13-18

Sometimes though, our friends are involved in some bad things. If they are it probably won't be long before you are as well, unless you do something about it.

1. The first thing you should do is make sure that you are right before God first. It is easy to disregard someone who rebukes you when you know they are seeped in sin as well.
2. Pray a lot that God will open the door and the right timing for you to speak to your friend.
3. Make sure you have thought about how to speak with kindness, gentleness and in a way that will least likely cause them to feel defensive. Help them feel safe and loved.
4. Be brave and go to them alone. It is easier to take a rebuke when you are not embarrassed because it is done in front of other people.
5. Be specific with facts rather than assuming their motives. For instance: "Do you remember when you were talking about so-and-so the other day? I don't know why you were saying those things, but I have noticed that you regularly talk about people behind their backs. I should not have been a part of that. I was wrong for listening, but I was hoping there could be a way that I could help you break the habit of being a gossip."
6. If they don't listen, than go through steps 1-3 and before step 4, bring a witness and then follow the progression of Matthew 18 by bringing it to an authority if they don't fix things.

Week Nine / Day Four: Friends

Proverbs 16:28, Proverbs 11:13, Proverbs 18:8, Proverbs 26:20

One very important thing to keep in mind when dealing with conflict and disagreements is to be careful of your friend's reputation. Do unto others as you would have them do unto you. A good name is rather to be chosen than great riches and if someone makes a mistake, it is very hard to overcome a bad reputation.

In fact, embarrassment and a bad reputation can cause pride to rear its ugly head and keep someone out of church for years. Remember to go to them alone and keep it quiet unless they are stubborn and unrepentant. Even then, leave it to your friend's authority to decide if it needs to be out in the open.

Gossipping is one of the most dangerous and destructive sins. It is the opposite of courage and honour. Grace is when we grant someone something they don't deserve. The honour of repenting of a sin without the whole world knowing about it is a grace we all would appreciate.

Week Nine / Day Five: Friends

1 Corinthians 5:7-13

I have had some great friends and some really bad friends. I am so thankful that God had my family move when I was a teen because I was already sliding down a slippery slope and making awful decisions with my life.

Separation from those influences saved me. If I had kept on that path, I am certain that I would not have my wonderful husband and five children who are being raised in a loving Christian home. I don't think I even knew today's passage was in the Bible, but I try to encourage people to read it and apply it in their friendships.

(We should be very careful to not be close friends with lost people. We will go over that next week.)

When it comes to un-repentant Christians, we are not to fellowship with them at all. If they have been through the steps listed earlier in the week and they refuse to change their sin, lovingly and carefully explain that in obedience to Scripture you need to stop hanging out with them until they repent.

Don't just stop hanging out with them without talking to them first. Don't seemingly randomly ignore them or give them the cold shoulder. Don't leave them confused. Let them know they are loved and you can't wait until the relationship is restored. Then regardless of how much it hurts, trust in God and obey His word.

Week Nine / Day Six: Friends

2 Corinthians 2:5-11, Matthew 18:21-35, Ephesians 4:29-32

Just as it is important to stand up for what is right and separate ourselves from some relationships regardless of how we feel, it is also important to learn how to forgive those who have repented.

Sometimes our friends just say something hurtful and then apologize later. Other times it is the friend who went wayward and has come back to the Lord and they need extra love and care.

While we might not always be the best of friends with someone who has repeatedly hurt us, we should always be willing to reach out and be an encouragement to them in their time of need.

You might just be the one who makes the difference they needed.

Week Nine / Day Seven: Friends

Proverbs 18:24

But maybe you find that you are struggling to make friends at all. You know that "a man that hath friends must show himself friendly," but when you try it just comes out all wrong. You feel like a reject.

I want to give you a brief outline of a video I did a while ago on [5]"How to Have More Friends." I hope it helps.

1. Don't expect to be part of an already existing tight-knit group of friends. They might already have too many friends to maintain or to want any new relationships.
2. Find people of similar interests and find opportunities to get involved in activities around those interests.
3. Choose kind people as friends. It is less likely they will be rude to you.
4. Learn "small talk skills." There are loads of books and videos on this topic.
5. Stop sharing your sob story. It is awkward for others and it is a hindrance to your growth as a person if you are bound by your past.
6. Give more than you get, but by your own strength of mind, not out of fear or to the extreme of being taken advantage of.

5Can be found at www.youtube.com/c/melissaschworer

Week Ten / Day One: Lost family

Galatians 6:7-10, James 3:13-18

Some people grow up in homes where everyone in their family is a Christian and so are their friends. Others grow up in an environment where they are the only person in their entire family who has ever accepted Christ as their Savior.

Today I want to give you some thoughts on how to treat lost family members.

The first thing we must be is patient. By this I don't mean that we should not speak up about Christ, but rather, don't get discouraged if they don't listen or seem as excited as you are.

I have seen people plant seeds about Christ in a relative's life and then years later it was someone else who led that person to the Lord. The neat thing is is that when they get saved, very often you will be one of the first people they call. They will remember your testimony and words.

But also in regards to patience, remember that they probably don't view sin how you do. If every time you see them you start pointing out their sins and how they are going to go to hell, it might not have the effect for which you had hoped.

Be very prayerful, cautious and gentle in how you approach people. Allow God to lead and to open doors.

Week Ten / Day Two: Lost friends

1 Peter 3:15, Psalms 1, Proverbs 1, Proverbs 24:1,2

While yesterday's principle applies to lost friends as well, I want to point out why we should separate from friends who are living wickedly.

The way of the wicked is the way of death and destruction spiritually and very often practically. And we will become like those with whom we associate ourselves.

It is possible to be a witness without hanging out with lost people doing what lost people do. I think about Jesus who did visit with the lost and ministered to them. But what people don't often point out is that he fellowshipped with the disciples and purposefully used his time with the lost to draw them to repentance.

When Jesus went to the house of Zacchaeus, the conversation centered around repentance. When Jesus spoke to Matthew the tax collector, Matthew left behind his old life and followed Christ. The adulterous woman was encouraged to sin no more. Mary Magdalene worshipped at Christ's feet. We just don't see Christ partaking in, or hanging out around sin without doing something about it. (Matt. 21:12-13)

The best way to be a light to the lost is to be as separate from sin as possible and full of hope in Christ.

Week Ten / Day Three: Lost co-workers

2 Timothy 2:20-21

I remember one time at work that I had two different pay settings. One for when I worked as a cashier and one for when I worked tables and got tips. Well, for a week or two they forgot to switch my pay scale on my paycheck and I was paid as a cashier and got my tips. I noticed it right away, but didn't say anything.

The Holy Spirit really started convicting me. Was God not my provider? Why didn't I just tell them? Then pride started kicking in. I was embarrassed that I hadn't said anything right away. What would they think of this "Christian" who had kept money that wasn't her own?

I could not bear the conviction and sheepishly approached my manager to fess up. They just said, "Thanks for being honest." and fixed it. Whether that made an impact on them or not made no difference. As a Christian I needed to do what was right because it pleased God.

Our cultures sometimes think that it is okay to compromise or sin a little so that the lost will know that we are sinners too and that we don't think we are better than them. It is as if "winning the lost at any cost" (which isn't in the Bible) means, "win the lost even if it means sinning to do it."

But first and foremost we were created to please God. Doing right must be about pleasing God. Winning the lost is important, but do it as a clean vessel, sanctified and fit for the Master's use.

Week Ten / Day Four: Lost neighbors

Luke 10:25-37, Proverbs 3:27

I live in a community where there are many LDS (Mormons). A lot of them are nice people and always willing to lend a helping hand.

It is hard to reach lost people who are great people, because honestly, sometimes they do more "good works" than I do. I get busy with my family and my church and I am "too busy" to help out anyone else.

But isn't that like the Levite in the story of the good Samaritan? He was too busy serving God to help anyone.

As I have grown in Christ, God has worked on me more and more about "good works."

I am not saying we are saved by good works, but that God still wants the Christian to do them. Look up the phrase "good works" in your Bible and see how often we are admonished to let our life be full of them.

When we are kind and reaching out to those in need, or even better yet, looking for needs, we will find that there are more opportunities to witness and share the gospel. We won't just be stuck on the hamster wheel of life.

Week Ten / Day Five: Lost leaders and politicians

1 Timothy 2:1-4, 2 Peter 2:9-11, Romans 13:1-8, Psalms 9:20

Whether you consider yourself political or not, our lives are very much limited or helped by our laws and leaders. I have read so much about history, the Federal Reserve, the United Nations and how it relates to communism and the one world government. As a result, I try not to ever watch the news. I find the world powers' disregard for God to be super discouraging.

What I do find encouraging is prayer and then hope of a quiet and peaceful life due to prayer. I pray that these rulers who hate God will know themselves "to be but men."

I pray that the Lord will raise up Daniels who won't compromise for any reason but have purposed in their heart that would not defile themselves and that God will put them near those in power.

I want to have respect for those in office, but not to be a "respecter of persons in judgment" (Deut 1:17, Prov. 24:23) so that I will be less easily deceived. I pray for each leader's heart regardless of their political party.

And while I may never speak to a president, politician, or public servant, I want to know that I have prayed for them sincerely and earnestly, because all power comes from God.

Week Ten / Day Six: Lost teachers

2 Timothy 2:23-26, 1 Timothy 6:20-21

If you are in a public school or college, chances are you will have a teacher who does not believe in God.

How are you going to deal with that? Do you know why you believe what you believe? Do you know Who God is and why creation is more scientifically valid than evolution? Your core beliefs will be challenged when you reach out to the lost.

Just the other day I was at an event with my husband. I had already seen these people a few times and had developed a rapport. This one person knew I was a Christian and had mentioned he was the kind of guy that the "Apostle Paul had said not to be around." I dug a little bit more and he said he was a "reformed evangelical and now an atheist."

I just kept listening and he said that when he was confronted with the book "The God Delusion" that he didn't have any proof to refute it and his faith was shattered. As I am not afraid of "science" because I have studied the Christian proofs quite a bit, I said, "The next time we have an event, I will have read the God Delusion and will give my honest opinion." I read the book and can't wait to talk to him when the opportunity arises.

My point is this, when it comes to lost teachers, be kind, honest, listen and treat them like you would like to be treated. No one wants to feel as if they are looked down upon. No one wants to be railed at or attacked personally because the other person can't hold their own when it comes to facts. Know what you believe, stick to the facts, be kind and be respectful and walk away from a lost cause.

Week Ten / Day Seven: The lost in our community

Galatians 6:9-10, Hebrews 6:10

The world does seem to get darker and darker. It can begin to feel like no matter how many tracts you hand out or how many times you have been involved in kindness evangelism that it doesn't make a difference.

I asked a missionary friend that exact question the other day. "Why?" "Why do we keep trying if no one listens?"

She said, "Because we are just one instrument in an orchestra and we have to play our part. We can only see our page, but the conductor sees the symphony."

Results are not up to us. Faithfulness is our responsibility. We can control whether or not we show up, but we cannot see how the seeds we plant are working.

Many stories have been told of missionaries who handed out tracts faithfully in one area of the country and then had come back for a visit many years later only to see a church had popped up and could be traced back to their toiling and sowing.

Keep on friends. Keep on. Go to college campuses, public streets, door to door and to everyone you meet and find some way to share the gospel. Be a seed planter and don't give up.

Part Three

Black, White & Gray Areas in Scripture

This section of the devotional was inspired when I asked a large group of young women this question, "What was the hardest thing you faced when you graduated high school and entered into independence?"

So many of them answered, "Figuring out what I believe and where to draw my lines on the gray issues in the Bible."

I asked them specifically what some of those areas were and I have listed most of them and more in this chapter. I also wanted to give you some more "black and white" questions and answers in regards to the fundamentals of faith and why we tend toward unity with some beliefs and separation with others.

Also, I wanted to provide you with some basic principles of discernment as you learn to go to the Scripture for all of your own answers to any new questions that face you.

All right. Does that all make perfect sense? Off you go to a little bit "meatier" teachings of the Bible. I know you can handle it.

Week Eleven / Day One: How does the Holy Spirit speak?

1 John 4:1-5, Matthew 7:15 - 20, Luke 6:43 - 45

We know that there is a spirit world and with those spirits come deception. We can be self-deceived and also led astray when we don't "try the spirits." When the "Spirit" or a "teacher" tells us something, we should do the following things before proceeding.

1. Check the emphasis.

   Are they pointing you to Scripture or toward some vague "leading of the Holy Spirit?" - John 14:26 and John 16:13

2. Check the fruits.

   Do those who practice or support the teaching show mixed fruit? They preach "Christ" and yet their disciples and churches continue to manifest the works of the flesh or a lack of separation? - Matthew 7:15 - 20, Luke 6:43 - 45 and Galatians 5:19 - 21

3. Check the doctrine and theology.

   Are the teachings supported by Scripture? - Romans 16:7-9

4. Check the life of any teacher.

   Are they living sinfully without any sign of repentance? Do they "profess" Christ and yet live in sin? (Hypocrites) - 1 Timothy 4:1-2

5. Check the teacher's stand on Christ.

   Do they profess that Jesus Christ was God who came down to earth in the flesh as the Messiah and Savior? - 1 John 4:1-5

God makes it clear that He puts His word above His very name. Remember, the Holy Spirit will never tell you something that contradicts Scripture.

Week Eleven / Day Two: He who has the most Scripture wins

2 Timothy 4:2-3

How doctrine affects our daily walk: "Biblical Living" has always been my strong point when it comes to understanding Scripture, but my husband is "Mr. Doctrine."

While I got "C's" in Bible Doctrine, he was getting an "A plus" and a note of commendation from his teacher. It was he who taught me the principle of "the weight of Scripture."

This means that if you imagine an old-school balancing scale and someone is trying to teach you a doctrine and they hand you some Scripture that you can't quite explain, you put it on the one side of the scale.

Then you put all the Scripture or evidence that you did understand and that supports the opposisng viewpoint. Each person would give all their Scripture and put it on their side of the scale and whichever side was "heaviest" with Scripture "wins."

For exampe, if one verse or passage makes you wonder about eternal security, but twenty verses support it, than chalk the one passage up to "I just don't understand that passage yet."

But don't throw out the "weight of Scripture" because of something you don't quite grasp.

Week Eleven / Day Three: Be willing to listen and learn

Proverbs 22:4, 2 Timothy 2:16, Titus 3:9, Romans 1:29

My biggest practical advice in regards to studying God's word and searching for the weight of Scripture and dealing with people with contrary beliefs is this: Humility. A wise man increaseth learning. A wise man loves the man that rebukes him. A wise man seeks truth.

The focus of "the weight of Scripture" is for biblical truth to "win" in your heart. If we are able to use truth to teach and disciple someone, that is a blessing, but God gives us a warning about "debate."

It is one thing to listen and glean and then go home and search it out in the Scripture. It is a whole other thing to stop listening and just try to prove why you believe we are right.

So, as you go on this journey of finding out why you believe what you believe, I want to remind you that sound wisdom and counsel is good, but more often than not you will need to be able to walk away from a heated conversation graciously.

It is a better choice to humbly agree to disagree if it is certain that each person is fully persuaded.

Week Eleven / Day Four: Doctrines that unite

2 Timothy 3:10 - 16

When it comes to our beliefs, there are some fundamentals that must be agreed upon or Scripture calls us a heretic. Do you know what they are?

1. The Deity of our Lord Jesus Christ (John 1:1, John 20:28, Hebrews 1:8-9).
2. The Virgin Birth (Isaiah 7:14, Matthew 1:23, Luke 1:27).
3. The Blood Atonement (Acts 20:28, Romans 3:25, 5:9, Ephesians 1:7, Hebrews 9:12-14).
4. The Bodily Resurrection (Luke 24:36-46, 1 Corinthians 15:1-4, 15:14-15).
5. The Inerrancy of the Scriptures themselves (Psalm 12:6-7, Romans 15:4, 2 Timothy 3:16-17, 2 Peter 1:20).

If someone does not believe these basics, they cannot be truly born again, but there are churches who profess Christ who do not believe these basics.

This is important, because if we do not make a distinction between a born-again Christian and someone whose religion merely involves Christ's name (but is based upon their church or their works) then many lost people will go to hell while still "professing Christ's name." (Matthew 7:21-23) Not all who call themselves "Christian" are saved.

Be courageous and loving and be willing to speak the truth in love to those who are caught in false doctrine and headed to hell.

Week Eleven / Day Five: Doctrines that divide denominations

Colossians 1:9-11, 1 Corinthians 3:1-3, Hebrews 5:13-14

As you grow in the knowledge of God and study to show yourself approved unto God, you will discover that salvation brings so many wonderful benefits. It is wonderful to belong to a church that will teach you the whole counsel of God.

This is when you will find that it is the truth and the goal of growing in Christ that will draw you to one church or another. That is not a contentious division, but rather a sweet unity of being like-minded with others around you and especially someone you might want to marry.

The reason I choose to be Baptist is their teaching on:

1. Baptism by immersion after profession of faith.
2. Priesthood of the believer. Confessing our sins to God alone and not a man.
3. Freedom to live according to one's conscience and the Bible as our final authority.
4. That I will never lose my salvation.
5. The signs of tongues and healings were for the Jews in Acts and not part of the New Testament Church as we know it.
6. Local church authority.

It would be difficult to sit under the preaching of someone who taught differently than what I can clearly understand from Scripture.

The moral dilemma is this: do we as Christians avoid these "divisive topics" or do we teach them anyway? Is all division wrong? Is all unity better? Should we just stick to the "milk of the word" or do we also teach the "meat?"

Week Eleven / Day Six: Biblical unity

Ephesians 4:1-16, Proverbs 27:17, Romans 12:18, 1 Timothy 4:1-2, 16

My favorite line of the song Onward Christian Soldiers is where it says, "One in faith and doctrine, one in charity."

I personally believe that if our spirits are humble and we are truly seeking the will and knowledge of God, that we can peacefully compare Scripture with Scripture with each other. Since the Bible is the final authority we can usually come to a basic agreement.

If we do not come to an agreement, then that might mean that there are limitations to our unity. It does not mean that one is a heretic and the other is the victor. Often it just means we will go to a different church with people with whom we are more like-minded. It doesn't mean we can't be friends or fellowship, but that our relationship might be a bit more shallow as we seek to live peacefully among men.

But then there are people with have known the truth and departed from the faith. What then?

Paul says that we should "take heed unto thyself, and unto the doctrine, continue in them: for in doing this thou shalt both save thyself, and them that hear thee."

Doctrine is key. Focus on learning and living doctrine.

Week Eleven / Day Seven: What do I mean by "living doctrine?"

Matthew 25:44-46, James 1:27

When I was in my first year of Bible College and just started to study things out on my own, I remember reading passages like today's and being completely confused.

I started to wonder if I had to help the sick or feed the hungry so that I could have eternal life.

I might have become the next Mother Teresa. What I did know is that there were many Scriptures that showed I had eternal securty, so that must have meant I just didn't understand this passage.

It was my husband who explained to me that Matthew 24 & 25 were talking about "the kingdom of heaven." (Matthew 25:1)

"What's the kingdom of heaven?" I asked. "That is the millenium." he replied. (If you don't know it yet, he has written several books on Revelation and The Kingdom.[6]) I was so excited to have him explain to me the difference between the Kingdom of God and the Kingdom of Heaven and see how God was not talking about me in Matthew 24.

You see how it could get confusing if you assumed that everything God said in the Bible applied to you. It could impact how you lived each day and cause you to live in error. Doctrine matters to everyday living. That is what the rest of this section of the devotional covers.

6Look on Amazon.com for books by Rick Schworer

Week Twelve / Day One: Precepts and commandments

Psalm 119:127 & 159, Joshua 22:5, Deut. 5:29

Yay! Commandments!

Commandments get a bad rap. It's like they have the reputation of sucking the fun out of life.

Some people look at them as if God wrote a letter that said,

"Dear Christian, I am holy. Therefore, everything that you can imagine to do for fun, I want you to know it's wrong.

That's all.

Enjoy your not fun life.

Sincerely,
God."

But the truth is that commandments teach us about how God would have us to love Him, how to love others, and honestly to protect us from hurting ourselves.

I know it is popular to say that God views all sins the same, and that might be true for a lost person but that is not true for the Christian.

This week I want to go over some commands that God says are such a big deal that if we broke them, He would want other Christians to break fellowship with us until we repent and change our ways.

Week Twelve / Day Two: Fornication

1 Corinthians 5:6-13

Fornication is the first sin that Paul names in this passage. He told the Corinthians to not keep company with fornicators. It is so important to note that he says that he doesn't mean lost people involved in this sin. He is specifically referring to saved people involved in it.

Christians are held to a higher standard, because they are temples of the Holy Ghost.

God says this is a sin that goes against our own bodies. (1 Cor. 6:18) and that we should flee from it (1 Cor. 6:18), abstain from it (1 Thess. 4:3), avoid it (1 Cor. 7:2) and repent of it (2 Cor. 12:21).

Paul also said that it is better to marry than to burn (1 Cor. 7:9). Therefore if this is an area of weakness for you, I would encourage you to commit to fighting this temptation daily, and also look to God and ask Him to provide you with a godly husband.

My advice to girls is to never, ever, ever be alone with a boy, because for some reason, no matter how good our intentions, our resolve seems to go out the window when temptations arise.

The best way to win over temptation is to flee from it and avoid it.

Week Twelve / Day Three: Covetousness

Psalm 10:13, Micah 2:2, Luke 12:15, Col. 3:5, Heb. 13:5

We don't talk very much about covetousness as a sin, let alone a sin that God abhors so much that He would cast a Christian out of fellowship for it.

To be honest, I always get a little fuzzy about what exactly covetousness is.

Here is the definition in the Webster's 1828 dictionary.

Inordinately desirous, excessively eager to obtain and possess, directed to money or goods, avaricious defined as "greedy of gain, immoderately desirous of accumulating property."

I think about gamblers, thieves, the mafia and cartels, those who desire to keep accumulating stuff even if it means spending more than they have, and lastly, I picture Scrooge.

Scrooge is like the man Jesus is describing in Luke 12:15. He has plenty enough to be giving, but refuses to help others at the risk of his own wealth.

Another covetous man would be a pastor, judge, king, politician or juror who refuse to be just because they are easily swayed by bribes or monetary gain.

To keep from this sin, we ought to check our hearts for its root: discontentment.

Week Twelve / Day Four: Extortion

Ezekiel 22:12, Matt. 23:25

Could you tell me what "extortion" is without a dictionary?

You might know it better as blackmail or by gaining something through threats.

Imagine a toddler throwing a tantrum. "I want that toy NOW!" or else. THAT is an extortioner. Now imagine that same child growing up to be a violent protester rioting in the streets.

Think now of teenagers demanding to get their own way or else they will "make their parents' lives miserable." Now imagine them at thirty with a gun robbing a gas station.

I envision corrupt tax collectors tearing apart people's houses and burning villages if people don't "pay up."

What about a person in church who says "If you don't let me have this position than I am going to split the church."

Jesus said in Matt. 23:25 that the Pharisees were extortioners. I wonder what they did. Maybe they would tell of the sins they knew if parishioners didn't pay money, kind of like absolutions of Catholicism.

They all have one thing in common: threats. Our example is Christ in 1 Pet. 2:23, Who, having the power of the universe, did not threaten but rather committed Himself to God.

Week Twelve / Day Five: Idolatry

1 Samuel 15:23, Col. 3:5, 1 Chronicles 16:25-26

When we think of idolatry we usually think of little Buddha statues, the virgin Mary and shrines filled with graven images.

Yet, God said that stubbornness is idolatry. I imagine it is because we worship our own will and way, more than that submitting ourselves to God's will and His authorities over our life.

Covetousness is also labelled as idolatry. Like stubbornness, covetousness causes us to be willing to disobey God's commands to fulfill our own desires.

There are many idols to which we give ourselves over: relationships, education, jobs, entertainment, sports, and vices.

There are so many things we allow to pull ourselves away from God as we lose our first love.

I am not sure at which point we are given over to idolatry in a way that is so noticeable people would say we are "overtaken in a fault" and try to restore us (Gal. 6:1)

But I would imagine that if we were confronted with Scripture and the process of Matt. 18 was fulfilled and yet we refused to part with our sin, it would definitely be the idol of stubborness.

Week Twelve / Day Six: Railing

1 Peter 3:9, 2 Peter 2:11, Jude 1:9

My pastor says that Christians have such a sense of right and wrong that we tend to lack mercy with others. Where an unsaved person might see someone sinning and just say, "Well, that's just how people are," a Christian sees it as an injustice.

In 2 Peter 2:11, God is describing rebels who despise the government and are casting railing accusations against them. This is in stark contrast to Paul (Acts 26:25) who said, "most noble Festus" and addressed a ruler with respect.

In Jude we see Michael the Archangel who would not dare to accuse the most guilty of all, Satan, but committed that judgment to the Lord.

There is a difference between meekly going to a person with a heart that desires restoration and intreating them with gentleness and peace versus lashing out accusations with malice.

But very often we have Christians proclaiming the faults of others (government officials, pastors, fallen Christians and such like) in public rather than following God's command to go to them privately.

Social media has made gossiping and railing part of our culture, but God says it should not be so.

Week Twelve / Day Seven: Drunkardneess

Deuteronomy 21:18 - 20, Proverbs 23:20-35

I have written an article at www.truthandsong.com called "Why Christians Don't Drink Alcohol" and it covers way more than what I could talk about in a daily devotional.

But I just can't help but think how yesterday I read an obituary of a grown man who took his life because he could not win the battle with alcohol. He had started as a teen and became the man in Prov. 23:35 saying, "when shall I awake? I will seek it yet again."

I began this week talking about how God's commands teach us to love Him, love others and protect our lives from evils. (Prov. 1:33)

This is one of those commands that are for our own protection. Wine is indeed a mocker. Strong drink is raging. Yet, many are deceived. So many are deceived and lives are destroyed.

Proverbs 31:5 truly says it so well, "Lest they drink and forget the law…"

And so, we conclude the six laws that I believe every Christian should take extra care to keep and the six sins they should flee.

Next week we will cover "Doubtful Things" and how to deal with gray areas in the Bible.

Week Thirteen / Day One: What is a doubtful disputation?

Romans 14:1-5

There were two things that I learned in my twenties that I wished I had learned a lot sooner.

The first was the ability to "agree to disagree" with someone, and the second was which areas of the Bible would cause "doubtful disputations." Agreeing to disagree happens when you have had a couple of (hopefully) peaceful discussions with someone and you have shown them Scripture or evidence on a topic and vice-a-versa and yet at the end of the discussions, neither of you is convinced by the other person's points.

I think about some very nice people who refuse to believe in the evidence for Intelligent Design and yet it would be counter-productive in the relationship to push the issue any further. And so, you just choose to not bring up the matter, and you choose to not harbor any ill will or contention.

The second is very similar but it usually about spiritual issues raised by cultural differences.

In verse five of today's daily Bible reading you will see the phrase "fully persuaded in his own mind." That is what your goal should be, to be fully persuaded about your beliefs.

When you are fully persuaded in something and you have all of the Scripture to back up your beliefs on cultural issues, you will find that it is much easier to agree to disagree and be charitable to those who differ.

Week Thirteen / Day Two: Days

Romans 14:6-10

There are things found in the Bible for which we are required to "spiritually judge" the matter and then there are things for which we are to not judge another Christian.

The specific ones we find in Romans 14 are specifically related to "days" and "religious practices" before a person was saved.

I want to talk a little bit about "days."

The more you study your history, the more you will find that nearly every day in the calendar has some form of pagan root.

For instance, Easter was a pagan holiday to celebrate the goddess of fertility, and yet in Acts 12:4, Easter was mentioned. But it did not seem to offend the disciples to acknowledge that Easter was existing at the same time as the passover.

Yet, there are some people who have been saved out of paganism, witchcraft, Luciferianism and Catholicism who are extremely convicted about celebrating certain holidays that they had previously used to worship their false gods.

Paul encouraged us out of love for others to be very discreet about our celebrations if they would offend a brother or sister in Christ. We are not to judge someone if we don't celebrate those days but others do.

Week Thirteen / Day Three: Stumblingblocks

Romans 14:11-15

Have you ever done a yoga stretch? I have. Then I watched a video about the roots of yoga and how it is used for worshipping the serpent god and that yoga classes are actually the most effective "evangelistic tool" for the new age movement.

Many yoga teachers actually consider themselves missionaries for their religion.

I was confused for a while about whether it was wrong to do certain stretches, and as I thought about it in regards to today's passage I realized that for me, I was not worshipping anything when I was doing certain hamstring stretches.

I was not engaging in meditative breathing or passive mental activities. I was just stretching. I felt like Paul. Stretching was not "unclean of itself" but I could certainly see how someone coming out of the new age movement would esteem yoga to be unclean.

But could I be mature enough not to put a stumblingblock in a brother's way? Could I avoid "doubtful disputations?" Could I be comfortable enough in my persuasion to just not do or talk about certain stretches if it offended someone's conscience? Or would I feel the need to convince them that I wasn't wrong in doing this exercise?

It is not about being a hypocrite. If they asked your opinion, be honest, but don't flaunt your liberty or God will hold you accountable for your lack of charity.

Week Thirteen / Day Four: Standards versus doubtful things

Romans 14:16-19

Can you think of some other areas that might cause conflict between Christians?

I sure can. I think I foolishly argued about them all.

But as we move into the next several weeks, I want to make it clear that there are "standards" for which the Bible doesn't draw any clear lines and then there are "standards" for which the Bible does state definitive ideas.

Not all standards are doubtful disputations, but they should all be treated with the same respect and charity in regards to conversation.

I think of how Paul says, "Let not then your good be evil spoken of:" and "Let us therefore follow after the things which make for peace, and things wherewith one may edify another."

If you live in a culture that says you should not reveal your ankles and yet there is no biblical precedent for that, esteem others better than yourself. Yield to your culture as you can (as long as it does not cause you to disobey Scripture).

If you find that a cultural yoke is too burdensome, then you have the liberty to move to a different region or church. The goal is respect and mutual submission in love.

Week Thirteen / Day Five: When liberty becomes sinful

Romans 14:20-23

It might seem like a pain to go the extra mile about something that you know isn't even a sin, but to God, it is a sin if you put a stumblingblock in front of a brother or sister in Christ.

In fact, if you cause a person to sin against their conscience (let's just say, they feel convicted about yoga and then do a few poses with you), God says they condemn themselves and that is evil for them.

Why would we ever want to cause someone to do an evil against God?

Usually it is because we are not comfortable enough with our own beliefs to be quiet about them. We feel the need to persuade others that we "aren't doing anything wrong."

But God would rather us just not flaunt our liberty. Paul says, "Hast thou faith? Have it to thyself before God." Don't publicize your celebrations if it is a hot topic in your culture.

If you feel the need to have a Christmas tree in Europe surrounded by converted pagans, keep it to yourself.

It's as simple as that.

Week Thirteen / Day Six: When liberty becomes sinful

1 Corinthians 8

This apparently was a big deal in the churches, because Paul addressed it more than once.

What is different in this passage versus Romans 14 is the fact that in 1 Cor. 8:12, Paul says that our putting a stumblingblock in front of a brother is actually a sin on our part against Christ.

We live in a society where we very much appreciate our liberty and not being under the law. I can imagine that the newly saved Jews felt the same way.

They were saved by grace and did not have to keep those stringent ceremonial laws any more. Yet, Paul knew that liberty could feed the flesh.

I would encourage you to remember that as we go through the next few weeks of examining our beliefs.

We ought always to be charitable and choose to sacrifice our own liberties if they are offensive in our circles, even if they have no biblical command against them.

Yet, we need to be fully persuaded and well studied about our beliefs, lest we find ourselves sinning in ignorance.

Week Thirteen / Day Seven: Yielding our liberties out of love

Colossians 5:13-15

Paul addresses the issue of liberty yet another time, and I feel ashamed how we as Christians are so prone to “biting and devouring one another.”

In this passage, if you read to the end of the chapter, Paul speaks about taking our liberty beyond doubtful things and rather sinning that grace may abound.

You see, we know that God is gracious and does forgive and that we are prone to wander.

Paul warns us to not take our liberty that far.

This is why it is important to know which issues are cultural and which issues are commands.

Either way, it is our responsibility to yield our liberties for the sake of our brothers and sisters in Christ; this is much easier said than done for sure.

Now moving on to drawing your own lines and standards according to Scripture.

Week Fourteen / Day One: What is modesty?

1 Timothy 2:9-10, 1 Peter 3:3

The issue of clothing has so many layers and they have to be addressed because there are so many sub-cultures within Christianity.

My goal is not to persuade you outside of Scripture, but to open your eyes to Scripture so that you can draw your own lines, because as someone once said, “If you don’t stand for something, you will fall for everything.”

The first Scripture that we see for the New Testament lady is the command for modesty. This emphasizes not drawing attention to what you are wearing, but letting your own life and works be the most outstanding thing about you.

This passage works hand in hand with Proverbs 31:30-31 where the emphasis is not upon the woman’s beauty, but rather upon her life and good works.

Websters 1828 dictionary defines modest as:
“Properly, restrained by a sense of propriety, hence, not forward or bold,” “Not loose, not lewd,” “not excessive or extreme, not extravagant.”

Propriety in this sense is in regards to being restrained by a sense of unity and oneness and not going outside your current cultural surroundings.

Can you imagine being in a town in the 1800’s and showing up in a red formal gown? I don’t care how little it revealed your shape, you would definitely be calling attention to yourself without a sense of propriety.

Week Fourteen / Day Two: Propriety and being appropriate

Deuteronomy 22:5, 1 Samuel 24:4, Proverbs 31:17

If you travel much, you are bound to have to ask yourself what this passage means to the New Testament lady, because it will become a matter of propriety.

Some people interpret this passage to mean nothing to today's Christian woman because it is given within a set of laws that are for the Jews alone.

Yet, as you look at society today with gender identity being an issue, it does make one wonder how God views cross dressing (as this Scripture is describing).

I am going to take some liberty and give you my thoughts. Imagine yourself as a missionary to China in 1890. Take a look around you and look and see what the men are wearing and what they women are wearing.

If you are a woman, it would make sense that you would choose to dress most like the women (Chinese jackets and trousers). That would not look like what American women wore, but it was appropriate to their culture.

If a male missionary went into the same culture, he should look at their attire (skirted robes) and be sure not to be "effeminate" (1 Cor. 6:9).

In doing so, you would be modest in both propriety and by not causing confusion about your gender in that culture. God is not the author of confusion and we should be clear to our culture that we are feminine.

Week Fourteen / Day Three: Femininity

Titus 2:5

We see one passage teaching us to not draw attention to ourselves through extravagant or lewd clothing, and we have another passage teaching us to be distinctly feminine in our culture. Next, in today's passage we have a general principle of being discreet and chaste.

Websters 1828 dictionary defines discreet as: "Prudent; wise in avoiding errors or evil, and in selecting the best means to accomplish a purpose; circumspect; cautious; wary; not rash."

Chaste is defined as: "Pure from all unlawful commerce of sexes. Undefiled. Free from obscenity."

That terminology kind of makes me laugh. "Commerce of sexes" means keeping anything sexual pure and within the bounds of marriage.

So, does that apply to your clothing?

I would assume so, as our clothing is how we express ourself to the world.

And so, are we cautious with our clothing? Are we circumspect as to how we are affecting those around us? Are we keeping the sexual parts of our body for our husbands alone? And does the Bible address which parts of the body those are?

We should definitely look at that, but first let's look at one more principle Jesus gives.

Week Fourteen / Day Four: Alluring attire

Matthew 5:27-28

This passage is extremely important because it shows that God holds us accountable again for being a stumblingblock. Just as doubtful matters are a sin against Christ if we cause someone to fall, so it is with our attire and allure.

This passage goes hand in hand with being discreet, cautious and circumspect.

I know that in our culture in the USA today, it is not a big deal to reveal our ankles, but in some areas of the world men have assaulted women because it was so physically enticing.

As all laws are covered under the law of "Love your neighbor as yourself" it would stand to reason that it would be charitable to examine our culture and not use our liberty to cause someone to lust.

That may be something you feel you cannot bear. If that is the case, I would encourage you to move to a different culture.

At the same time, some cultures promote attire that is revealing beyond Scriptural bounds. In that case, the Bible's more strict standard ought to be your guide.

Do you know which Scriptures address what God views as sexual or naked in nature?

Let's look.

Week Fourteen / Day Five: “Uncovering nakedness”

Leviticus 18 & 20, Exodus 28:42, Isaiah 47:2,3

When you study Scripture, it is important to put it in context and when the Bible talks about “uncovering nakedness” it is in a sense of shame and sin.

When I first studied modesty, I had to ask myself if God has a view of what nakedness is that surpasses just the Jewish law.

It is good to note that in Isaiah, while the description of uncovering nakedness has nothing to do with law, it has everything to do with what God views as nakedness and shame.

God does not give many clear lines about attire, but He does give a few.

This is one of them.

The next one again has nothing to do with a command about clothing, but again is more of a principle for which the Christian must discern God’s view on the topic.

Week Fourteen / Day Six: Sensuality

Proverbs 5:15-21

I don't know if I will ever be old or mature enough to not feel a bit silly when I read this passage of Scripture. It's just awkward, but it does hold some truth for men and women.

It puts this area of your body in the context of marriage and not for "strangers with thee."

You will never find a verse that says, "Thou shalt not show cleavage."

But God speaks of being discreet, circumspect, chaste and not to cast a stumblingblock for another brother and this passage puts God's view of what areas of your body are to be for marriage alone.

Week Fourteen / Day Seven: Culturally aware

Proverbs 7

There are only about four to five times in the Bible where it specifically speaks of the attire or apparel of a woman.

This is one where we can learn what not to do. This is a matter of cultural separation as well as being discreet and chaste in your clothing.

In the Old Testament (Gen. 38:15) what signified a harlot was that she covered her face. Is it a sin to cover your face? Not at all.

In Papua New Guinea, the mistresses would wear long straight skirts. Are straight skirts a sin? Nope. But the local woman would only wear long full skirts because they did not want to be identified with a loose woman.

When I was young, a harlot would wear stiletto heels, fishnet stockings, a lycra mini skirt and bright red lipstick. Now, I see women in church doing the same.

We can learn from this. (1 Thess. 5:22)

As we conclude this week, I hope you were able to make some decisions about what God would have you to wear.

Week Fifteen / Day One: Two types of music

Exodus 15:20, 21 and 32:17-19, Psalm 40:3

I wanted to start here because it is the first time we hear of singing in the Bible and it contrasts two types of music.

While I don't know exactly what this music sounded like in Exodus, I do know this:

In Exodus 15

1. They used a timbrel (which is a percussion instrument)
2. The ladies danced with the ladies and sang songs of praise to God.

In Exodus 32

1. It sounded like shouting and like the tribal war cries.
2. It was done by people who were naked.
3. It was associated with idolatry.

I guess what I want you to notice from the start is that not all music is the same and by their fruits you shall know them.

Week Fifteen / Day Two: How music can be used

Ephesians 5:19, Colossians 3:16, James 5:13, Hebrews 2:12, Psalm 40:3, 2 Sam. 22:50

The Old Testament has so much to say on music regarding how it was used in their cultures, and how the difference between how God's people used it and how the pagans used it.

But concerning the purpose of music for the New Testament Christian, God gives us a few purposes for music found in these Scriptures.

1. Singing to the Lord.
2. Speaking to one another.
3. Admonishing one another.
4. Teaching one another.
5. Expressing a merry heart.
6. Singing at church.
7. Turning the heathen to God.

The type of music God mentions are "psalms, hymns and spiritual songs."

Now there is no time period of when these songs should be written, just that these are the types we should sing.

In these passages the purposes of music are directed mostly by their lyrics, but I couldn't help but wonder if God said anything about music without lyrics, like did He address cultural music and instrumental?

So, we'll explore more tomorrow. I hope this is making you think.

Week Fifteen / Day Three: Music without lyrics

Daniel 3:5-7, 1 Sam. 16:23, 2 Sam. 6:5

Honestly, there is not much about music without lyrics except these passages.

In Daniel we see that when the music was played, people were to bow down to a false god.

In the two passages in Samuel we see that when David was a skilled instrumentalist and when played he played the harp for Saul it drove away evil spirits.

I guess what I take away from this is that God can use instrumental music and so can Satan.

This leaves me with the questions of: "Is music neutral? Is it how we use it that defines if it is good or bad?"

This leads me to two unique passages that I would have never noticed had I not searched the Scriptures for every mention of "musick," songs, instruments, sing and those variations.

I hope you think these next two passages are as interesting as I did.

Week Fifteen / Day Four: Singing in the ways of the Lord

Psalms 138:4-5, Amos 5:14-23

Did you see in Psalms 138 how when all the kings of the earth sang that they sang "In the ways of the Lord." They didn't sing "of" the ways of the Lord but "in" the ways of the Lord.

If God has a preference, I wonder if we can tell what it is.

In Amos 5:23 we can see one preference of God about music. He hates it when praise is sung to Him when the singer is living a life of sin. In this passage we see the words "hate," "despise," "will not accept" and "will not hear" in regards to their worship.

This is consistent to His thoughts about rejecting other forms of worship when it is done outside of "the ways of the Lord." Like when He killed the men who offered a strange fire on the altar (Lev. 10:1,2). Also the men who steadied the Ark of the Covenant when it was transported outside of God's particular command. (2 Sam. 6:5-14), and also God's preference for a particular altar in Josh. 22, 1 King 12:27-30, 2 Kings 18:22 and 2 Chron. 32:12.

It appears God's prerequisite for accepting music and worship is that it be done in obedience.

Which is what Samuel said to Saul in 1 Sam. 15:22 when Saul tried to worship and sacrifice to God while being in rebellion to God's commands.

And so, before we use music for its intended purposes, let's look and see if there is something God wants us to do before we sing praises to Him.

Week Fifteen / Day Five: A heart of repentance and worship

Matt. 5:23, Psalm 66:18

There are two major things that we need to do before we sing to the Lord or try to glorify Him in music.

The first is that we need to make things right with an offended brother or sister in Christ.

The issue of unforgiveness and bitterness is something that will defile many and God tells us to go to our brother if there is ought between us and them.

The second is the issue of an unrepented iniquity.

God said that if we love Him we should keep His commandments and when we are purposefully sinning and refusing to get it right, He takes it seriously. If people take the Lord's supper with sin in their lives, they are in danger of sickness and in other cases, death (1 Cor. 11:29, 1 John 5:16)

This all hearkens back to the music in Amos 5:15-23. Music should come from a clean life and a clean heart.

Week Fifteen / Day Six: Separation from evil associations

2 Cor. 6:14-18

Another thing that the Christian should look at in their music is how separated it is from the music of the unsaved in your culture. There are so many cultures around the world. Some examples are:

1. Traditional Asian folk music with the "guzheng" is completely different than the "oem" sounds and rhythm used to worship buddha. As a Christian, I would steer as far away from the "oem" or anything that produces a passive mental state as I could.
2. The Native American has their shamman music and "saman" comes from the Tungas word "one who knows or knows the spirits."
3. VooDoo music originating from western Africa comes from the word "vodun" which means "drum and spirit." Its uses have all been to call the power of devil.
4. Traditional Jewish music is tricky because in the 1700's the Jews integrated Kabbalah worship into their religion and the majority of Jews became Hasidic. Their music took an African / Middle eastern / mystical sound to it. On the opposite end there is the European influence and the polka march that westerners associate with Hebrew music. With that in mind I would steer away from their "spiritual music" and lean toward their folk music.
5. Rock and Roll originated in America in the 1920s with blues, jazz and swing.

You can learn more about this history through my video series on Youtube: What Does God Say About Music?

Week Fifteen / Day Seven: The appearance of evil

1 Thess. 5:22, Matt. 7:15-20, Luke 6:43-49

There are two final principles for the Christian that I would like to mention in regards to a heart of obedience before God and how that impacts music.

Yesterday we talked about separating from music that is associated with sin, calling evil spirits or worshipping idols.

Today I want to point out that God wants us to not only separate from evil, but also that He wants us to abstain from any appearance of evil. If we are listening to music that would cause someone to wonder if we are listening to music associated with devils and sin, God says to abstain from it.

Lastly, you might wonder, “Well, how do I know for sure if something is evil?” I would encourage you to do as Jesus said. He encouraged us to examine the fruit of something and if it is evil, to cut it off. Keep in mind that God’s word will not return void no matter if it is mixed with sin. An evil tree will always produce evil fruit and a good tree will always produce good fruit, even if they are planted in the same orchard. Check the fruits of the music.

I did a fascinating study on the fruit of classical music, rock and roll, new age meditative music and tribal rhythms. You would be amazed at what follows these musics in each culture in which they make an appearance.

I hope this information reaches ears that hear and a conscience that is tender as you decide for yourself from what music you should separate, abstain or participate.

Week Sixteen / Day One: How media affects our heart

Psalm 101:2-4

I have to admit it. One of the things that I struggle with is media. Media is my entertainment and at times it really does cleave or cling to me.

I define media as movies, tv, blogs, websites, video games and social media.

I really have to be careful about not only the content of what I view, but also how it affects my heart and mind, and then on top of that I have to monitor how much I ingest.

Is it just me, or can you relate?

This passage of Scripture truly is my guide in regards to my media consumption. I try to walk with a perfect heart that wants what God wants. I try to ask myself, "Is this wicked according to the Bible?" And then when I know that something does not meet that standard, I go a step further and ask, "Do I hate the work of them that turn aside? Or do I love it and allow it to cling to me?"

And so this week, while I am not going to tell you where to "draw your lines," I want to give you some Scripture that relates to common themes found in media.

Week Sixteen / Day Two: The spirit of fear

2 Timothy 1:7

You know what was so confusing to me when drawing my own lines about what I watched? I struggled with consistency.

I mean, if I was going to set no wicked thing before my eyes, was there any difference between detective shows and gore? Weren't they all about murder and intrigue? Is there a difference between watching an act of violence versus a story where people are fighting against it?

What I did know was this, "God hath not given us the spirit of fear" and the spirit of fear is demonic. While I do have some specific things I don't watch because of that, it is a question I really had to examine.

I mean, if Jesus is the light and men love darkness rather than light, then what does that mean for the Christian?

Should I just skip an entire genre of movies because I am a Christian? Or is it a matter of the content within the movie?

I tend to try to stay as far from a questionable line as possible just to be safe, but as you are drawing your own lines, please pray and search the Scriptures for what God sees as dark or fearful.

Also, be aware that once a door is open to demonic influence it isn't easy to close it, especially if something cleaves to us.

Week Sixteen / Day Three: Witchcraft

2 Chron. 33:6, Gal. 5:20, Lev. 19:31, Lev. 20:6, Deut. 18:11

Christians cannot deny that God wants us to avoid witchcraft, but it seems everything has some form of "magic" in it. Some is just imagination and some has to do with sorcery, incantations, spells, chanting and necromancy.

If you don't draw a line somewhere on this, you will for sure find yourself allowing things that God condemns. If you don't stand for something, you will fall for everything.

I would encourage you to take a more objective view about this topic. Rather than looking at it in regards to "how it affects you," I would ask you to look at it along the lines of how close it is to what Scripture condemns.

Because God hates real witchcraft.

So some questions you can ask yourself are these:

1. Is magic shown as good or evil in this media?
2. How close to true witchcraft is this? Could I model something similar and perform a spell myself?
3. Are there sorcerers and witches or is this imagination?
4. Are they dealing with familiar spirits and demonic powers?
5. Is this involving necromancy (communicating with the dead)?
6. Does this involve occult symbols and practices?
7. Does it portray white versus dark magic? Is that okay?

Be sober about this topic especially. This type of media opens spiritual doors into your home and heart.

Week Sixteen / Day Four: Fornication

1 Cor. 6:18, Gal. 5:19, Eph. 5:3, 1 Thess. 4:13

I was watching a film by some Christians and there was a moment when the leading man and leading woman were about to kiss and I almost panicked because I knew both of them personally. And one was married to someone who wasn't the leading lady.

I gasped, "Oh no! He's not going to kiss her is he? His poor wife!"

Now, they didn't kiss, but imagine if they did. This wife and her little kids would feel awful and everyone at their church would wonder about "the kiss."

But people do that all the time in movies and we don't think about it as God sees it. We just consider they are playing a role or take for granted that movie stars have awful marriages, they are unfaithful to their spouses and they aren't Christians, therefore it is okay.

But in Prov. 5:15-21 God shows how the marriage bed is not for "strangers" and that includes ours and theirs.

There is no such thing as a "pretend kiss" in Hollywood and there is no "pretend nudity" as well. They are really happening. We cannot deny that when we are watching people kiss and perform romantic or sensual scenes that it is indeed sin before our eyes.

When the Bible says, "I will set no wicked thing before mine eyes" where will you draw your lines on fornication?

Week Sixteen / Day Five: Communications

Eph. 4:29, Col. 3:8, 1 Pet. 1:15, 16, Ex. 20:7

Man, this one is not easy. It seems like cursing is in everything. It's in books, on blogs, in cartoons, memes and music.

But our communications aren't just about cursing. Media is full of railings, lies, slandering, tail bearing, gossip and filthy innuendos.

Sometimes I have felt like there is nothing edifying for the Christian out there.

There is no doubt that wicked communications are sinful, but I mean, at this point you are probably thinking, "Is there any media appropriate for a Christian?" I don't want you to shy away from that question, because it is something you have to answer.

For me, I have found that there are businesses that filter movies and sites that review book content and they have been a blessing to our family, but there were years when our family was trying to answer the question above and we didn't ingest very much until we were fully persuaded of a solution.

We all have to stand before God and in Prov. 5:21 it says that "the ways of man are before the eyes of the LORD, and he pondereth all his goings."

It is good to make your own decisions and draw lines with the fear of the Lord in mind, that is the beginning of wisdom. You can never go wrong that way.

Week Sixteen / Day Six: Moderation

Eph. 5:15-17, Phil. 4:5, 1 Cor. 9:25-27, Gal. 5:22-24

This one kills me. It took me a long time to detach myself from loving the pleasures of entertainment more than I loved God. I mean, I went from having no standards to drawing clear lines with conviction, but it wasn't painless.

At this point, I don't struggle so much with setting sinful things before my eyes anymore, but I do struggle with serving God with my time rather than wasting away in front of a screen.

And so I have learned to budget my time. I tell my time where to go rather than wondering where it went. It isn't a fail safe, but it helps.

I try to set priorities and goals for life, and then make time for what is good.

But there is a whole section of this devotional dedicated to that and so, for now, we will move forward.

Week Sixteen / Day Seven: Guarding your heart

Jeremiah 17:9, Daniel 1:8, Psalm 37:4, Prov. 4:23, Col. 3:2, 1 John 2:15, Rev. 2:4

Because this is such an area of weakness for us, I want to conclude this week focusing on the heart.

If you have no heart to serve the Lord, this whole discussion will do very little.

I look at the life of Daniel and see how three whole kingdoms passed and he was just faithful. His loyalty was with God and his life made a difference. I want my life to make a difference and I hope you do too.

But if we are not purposed in our heart that we will not defile our lives with even the simplest of things (in Daniel's case it was food), than we will find it hard to be purposeful to obey God when the storms of life come upon us.

Are we to be as the wise man who built his house upon the rock, or will we be led astray by our heart's desires and live on sinking sand? Our lives will reflect those choices.

Each verse in today's bible reading speaks to what God wants of our hearts and it will help you as you make decisions in regards to how God views what you set before your eyes.

Week Seventeen / Day One: Should I hang out there? Karaoke

Hosea 4:6

I remember while I was in Bible college I went with a friend to do karaoke. It was a little bit strange because even though I wasn't drinking and I still was unconvinced about my music standards, it was in a bar environment and that felt weird.

I had never really thought before about whether it was wrong.

I guess it was one of those situations where I grew up in an environment where my parents did not do that type of thing and I never had really thought before about whether it was wrong.

We have gone over quite a bit of Scripture by now and throughout this week I want to call upon the knowledge you have gained.

So, rather than giving specific Scriptures, I want to teach you how to make your own decisions, by asking you to call upon biblical standards.

1. Would the music be in line with the Bible's purpose and standards of separation?
2. Does the environment abstain from the appearance of evil in my culture?
3. Will this in no way be a stumblingblock for my companion?
4. Would this honor God and His word?
5. Would this feed my spirit?
6. Would I be free from fleshly temptations?

If the answer to each of those questions is "Yes" than proceed. You have biblical liberty.

Week Seventeen / Day Two: Should I hang out there? Dances

Exodus 15:20 & 21, Exodus 32:16, Judges 21:16-25, 1 Sam. 18:6, 2 Sam. 6:16, Psalm 149:3, Psalm 150:4

I always laugh a little when studying dancing in the Bible because of the passage in Judges 21:21. I am so glad I do not live in a culture where men steal women and make them their wives. That was a time when every man did that which was right in their own eyes.

Since then, God has given us His written word and the Holy Spirit to live within us. So, what can we glean about dancing from the Bible and how does that apply to us?

When I look at these Scriptures I can see that not all dancing is wrong. I wish I could go back in time and see what these dances before the Lord looked like, don't you?

I did notice that in Exodus 15:20 the women danced with the women and in 2 Sam. 6:16 David danced all by himself. These dances don't seem to be like the dances of our culture today and are consistent with 1 Cor. 7:1 where a man is not to touch a woman who is not his wife.

And so when making a decision about dancing you can't just rely on a "Thou Shalt Not Dance" from the Bible. You are going to have to use some precepts or guidelines from throughout Scripture, just like we did with karaoke.

Go back to yesterday's questions and ask them as they relate to dancing.

Week Seventeen / Day Three: Should I hang out there? Movie Theaters

Phil. 4:8, Romans 1:28-32, Eph. 5:6-13

This may seem silly to some of you, but I know that when my mom was growing up it was a huge deal to go to the movie theatre. She was not permitted to do so.

In fact, some still do not attend the movie theater.

The movie theater is kind of like a beach. There is sin and nudity everywhere, but what if what you are doing is not wrong?

The first thing you need to come to terms with is whether you believe watching movies is wrong or if it is just the content. The verses I gave today are the verses I have seen that can refer to movies in general.

When it comes to what you are watching at the movie theater, if you believe that content is the deciding factor than I guess if you go in after the previews and you have checked the content advisory, you could come out unscathed.

Then there is the question of consistency. Do you watch movies at home unfiltered but you won't go to the movie theater? Is there any difference? Is there any Scripture that could help you clear this up? Is there something innately wrong with the movie theater itself?

So, go back to day one of this week and go through the questions listed and be fully persuaded one way or another.

Week Seventeen / Day Four: Should I hang out there? Bars, Parties and Clubs

Prov. 23:20-35, Romans 14:21, Prov. 20:1, Hab. 2:15, Eph. 5:18

Here are some things that the Bible associates with drinking and the bar, party and club lifestyle.

- Strange women and whores (Prov. 23:26, 33)
- Sorrow and sadness (Prov. 23:29)
- Fights and contention (Prov. 23:29)
- Physical impairments (Prov. 23:29, 34)
- Death and poisoning (Prov. 23:32)
- Perversion of your heart (Prov. 23:33)
- Loss of memory (Prov. 23:34)
- Injuries (Prov. 23:34)
- Addiction (Prov. 23:34)
- Women being taken advantage of (Hab. 2:15)
- Foolishness (Prov. 20:1)
- Casting a stumblingblock (Rom. 14:21)

There is no scripture in the Bible that says "Thou shalt not drink" but it does say not to go to seek mixed wine or the wine that moves itself aright. This is a strong admonition of Solomon (the wisest man in the Bible outside of Christ) to his son in regards to the drinking lifestyle. It would be unwise to disregard its context and become one who is deceived and mocked by wine and strong drink.

So, if the Old Testament says not to look upon the wine when it is red and when it moves itself aright, describes the drunk who goes to seek mixed wine, tells us not to get drunk in the New Testament and to avoid it if it is a stumblingblock, then one can reason that drinking and its associations are not for today's Christian.

Week Seventeen / Day Five: Should I hang out there? Hookah / Vaping / Tobacco / Cannabis Bars

2 Cor. 6:14-18, 1 Cor. 9:25-27

God says a lot about drinking, but not a lot about smoking. In fact, there was a time in our culture where nearly everyone smoked. Is it possible for something to not be a sin and then to become a sin even if the Bible doesn't mention it specifically?

Before we knew the effects of these products upon our bodies this question could probably be put under "doubtful things." Since then, we have learned of cancer, damage to blood vessels and brain cells. Generally, they would be put on the same plain as gluttony.

But there are some other Scriptures that make us question as well. Should Christians separate themselves from these things due to the lifestyle of those with whom these products are associated?

Also, we as Christians need to look at the issue of being controlled by a substance in both the addictive sense and the altered state of our consciousness and decision making.

Scripture seems to give general principles on this topic and I hope this was a help.

Week Seventeen / Day Six: Should I hang out there? Casinos

Prov. 28:20, 1 Thess. 5:22, Luke 16:1-13

So when my friend got married we crossed into Canada to visit a casino. We were eighteen and we weren't going to gamble. I think we got an ice cream cone and came home.

Why is it so exciting to go places and do things that are "forbidden?" Is it curiosity? I don't know, but I remember the thrill of going there.

My husband's father was a twenty-one dealer who grew up in Las Vegas. He and his wife got saved when my husband was four and one day they were driving by a billboard featuring a dancer and, as a little boy, my husband asked, "What's that lady doing?"

To which they responded, "That's no lady and this is no place to raise a family."

It's a funny story today, but previously they lived the Las Vegas lifestyle and they knew the evils firsthand.

Today I would go back to day one of this week's devotion and ask myself those questions before I naively fulfilled my curiosity on something questionable. Those questions haven't guided me wrong so far.

Week Seventeen / Day Seven: Should I hang out there? When in doubt … don't.

Galatians 5:21

A pastor once said something very wise that stuck with me. If you are a point where you or someone else is asking, "Well, what's wrong with …?" You should turn around and ask yourself, "What's right with it?"

Honestly, I can't cover every situation that our sinful world will use to entice our flesh. I think this is why Paul said the term "and such like." We tend to know what is evil or perceived as evil in our cultures. We know what we should avoid, but we try to find ways to excuse them anyway.

So many times we do things just to fulfill the lusts of our flesh.

I know I have and at times still do. Right now, I am thinking of that dessert bar that led me into gluttony. No, I am serious. Today's passage speaks of "revellings" and those were gluttonous feasts. I struggle with that at times.

By the end of this week you might wonder, "Well, than what *can* the Christian do for fun?" I asked myself that question as well. I came to the conclusion that the best form of fun for the Christian is recreation.

Snowboarding, skiing, hiking, biking, swimming, weight lifting, canoeing, rafting, fishing, boating, taking walks, staring at the stars, sports and "the such like." There is so much we can do, so don't be discouraged.

Run the race that is set before you and "Keep on!"

Part Four

Values, Priorities and Stewardship

I have to admit that I tend to be a perfectionist and I read all the articles and watch the videos that talk about "My Morning Routine" or "10 Habits of Highly Successful People" and anything that will give me an advantage at making the most of my time.

I believe that we accomplish those things that we make part of our daily routine.

Stewardship is entirely about those practical daily routines. Sometimes they can become boring. At times they are down right difficult to continue. But those things that we value and make a priority in our life will be seeds that we plant and that will grow in time.

But as I am just now seeing how many of those around me are finding their lives crumbling around them, I look with sadness and wish they would have a heart for God's word and God's ways.

The rain falls on the just and unjust alike, and those lives built upon the sure foundation and principles of the Bible seem to require more patience to see good fruit.

Those who seek riches, influence and the pride of life spring up and cause us envy, but if you choose to not be weary in well doing you will indeed reap if you faint not.

Don't be discouraged. Find God's values. Choose what it will take to accomplish a fruitful life of righteousness and charity. Set your daily life priorities in order and Keep On.

Week Eighteen / Day One: Our heart

Matthew 6:21, Proverbs 16:9, Proverbs 4:23

This last section of this devotional is dedicated to self-management, also known as our stewardship.

The other day I was leading the songs in Jr. Church and I always want people to understand what they are singing. So, I asked, "What is the difference between 'Jesus Loves Me This I Know For The Bible Tells Me So' and 'Jesus Loves Me This I Know Because I Feel It This Is So'?" I was trying to point them to confidence in the Bible and that we should not follow our heart, but follow after truth.

A girl who was newer to church raised her hand and said, "But shouldn't we follow our passions?"

I understood what she meant. I explained to her that I can follow my passions as long as they are in line with Scripture. For instance, if I am passionate about my husband, than I should pursue that, but if I am passionate about someone else's husband I should not pursue that.

If I did, then it would lead to divorce, children in a broken home, God's name and reputation would be marred and I would not be pleasing to God as He said, "If ye love me, keep my commandments."

She said, "Well, my parents are getting divorced and it's not for any of the reasons you mentioned. My dad is gay and God doesn't say it's wrong and my mom's boyfriend is religious and wouldn't it be better if everybody was true to their self?" ... continued tomorrow

Week Eighteen / Day Two: Our heart

Jeremiah 17:9-10, Psalm 37:4

After her newer question, I looked at my husband, because this had gone a little further than I intended as we were just singing "Jesus Loves Me", but he said, "Go ahead."

I then carefully and discreetly explained what I shared with you guys a few weeks ago about what God says about same gender relationships and how even if our heart says one thing, we should obey the Bible.

She looked at me and quickly replied, "Well, I know God doesn't like it, but I still believe that my dad should do what he thinks is right."

I can't count how many times I have carefully explained something with Scripture or explained creation with science and had someone respond with, "Well, I see the evidence, but I believe ..."

My point is this, we must choose for our heart's desires to be wrapped up in the Lord's truth and the Bible's direction. We must trust it more than we trust ourselves.

Because there may come a day when what we want so desperately is just a teensy bit off from God's word and we justify why it's okay to compromise just a little.

What a slippery slope that becomes.

You are to be a steward of your own desires. Guard your heart carefully, because it will direct your paths.

Week Eighteen / Day Three: Wisdom

Proverbs 2:4, 2 Chronicles 1:11, Colossians 2:3, 2 Timothy 2:15

The Bible's emphasis on wisdom's value is stated over and over throughout the Proverbs.

I can't help but think of the story of Solomon and how he did not ask for riches, power, honour, long life nor the life of his enemies. God was moved by what Solomon considered a treasure, and you may already know the rest of the story is that God granted Solomon that gift.

Solomon is deemed as the wisest man in the Bible and he spent so much time imparting to us that wisdom.

I can't help but think about how God asked us to study to shew ourselves approved unto Him.

How is your stewardship of God's word? Do you actively seek to understand it, or are you just reading it to check it off your list of things to do? If you have gotten this far in this devotion, I would say that you are getting a good start. Keep learning and keep growing.

Week Eighteen / Day Four: Wickedness

Proverbs 10:2, Micah 6:10, Proverbs 2:17

I know it is unconventional to have "wickedness" as one of the treasures of the heart, but the Bible mentions it and I would be unwise to not emphasize what God emphasizes.

I read in a [7]book on soul winning that the author was good friends with Charles Barkley and had played with him in the NBA. But after his salvation this author had changed his ways.

He was determined to try to tell his lost basketball friends about the gospel and on one occasion was sharing the gospel with Charles Barkley's brother. The brother explained how he did not want to get saved because he enjoyed the partying, the women, the money and the freedom that sin gave him.

I know a few Christians who like the strange woman have forsaken the God of their youth for similar treasures of wickedness.

Sometimes our treasures are just a little bit skewed and sometimes they are all the way into wickedness. I guess a good thing to ask is which direction are you looking? Are you asking "What's so wrong with ...?" or are you asking, "What's good and right that I can do?"

7One Thing You Can't Do In Heaven, Mark Cahill

Week Eighteen / Day Five: Money

Proverbs 21:6, Hebrews 11:26, 1 Timothy 6:10, Matthew 6:24

It has been said that the Bible has more to say about money management than it does many other topics. As I wrote an entire book[8] on the topic, I can say for sure that it says quite a bit. But money is a tricky issue, because you need money to survive.

In fact, if you aren't fully prepared to provide for yourself as a single person or to live on a single income in marriage, you can find yourself much like the peasant during the medieval times who just works and works and still falls short of being financially independent, living in perpetual servitude.

On the flip side we are told that we are not to labor to be rich or to lay up treasures for ourselves on earth. Where do we find that balance?

I honestly think it is a heart issue. We should do our very best to be wise learners and learning a skill is a biblical admonition, but if our motive is to please God and do all to His glory then we will be less likely to compromise.

When I was young, I committed to put church attendance before work. At places where the application said, "You must be able to work during open hours" I still listed that I could not work on Wednesdays or Sundays due to religious beliefs.

I was hired at multiple places and was never required to work during church hours. I never compromised when offered "extra hours if I could work on Wednesdays." You see, I knew that God was my Provider and that He could make up the difference.

8Faith and Finance – Peace With or Without Prosperity can be found at www.amazon.com or www.truthandsong.com

Week Eighteen / Day Six: Love

Proverbs 16:3

We have talked about relationships extensively, but I want to cover the subject here in a different context.

It is so easy to fall in love, but not so easy to stay in love. That is because when love is a feeling it can change from moment to moment. But when love is a choice, it can override feelings.

The other day I was talking to a man whose wife was expecting their first child and it was a girl. He said, “I hope I can have three girls so that I can spoil them.” I have three girls and I immediately thoughts, “Oh! That is a bad idea.”

I said, “As someone who is raising three girls, I would encourage that you don’t spoil them but rather teach them two things: 1. The world doesn’t revolve around them, and 2. Don’t live according to their feelings but live according to truth.”

When that feeling of love overrides good decision making we can get ourselves into a lifetime commitment of trouble.

If you talk to several married individuals, who have good marriages, about a guy you like or are interested in and the majority of them give you words of caution or some dire perspective of where marrying that person might take you, you probably need to make a “head choice” rather than a heart choice.

Be a good steward of who you choose to love.

Week Eighteen / Day Seven: Our success

Joshua 1:8-9, 1 John 2:16, Ecclesiastes 12:13

The idea of success is something we hear a lot about. I am even developing an online [9]course of how to successfully step out on your own. We want to be good at what we do. We want to know we are not wasting our time. I get it.

But to be honest, the issue of "the pride of life" is an area where I regularly have to check myself. Am I willing to write a song for the Lord alone? Am I willing to play the piano for church and hope not to be noticed? If I plant seeds of truth and see it fall on hard soil, should I quit? If my children turn from God, but I have been faithful am I a failure? What is success anyway?

I have stated this many times throughout this devotional, but success is fulfilling our purpose of pleasing the Lord with our lives. The best way to do that is to love the Lord with all our heart, minds, and strength. And the best way to love the Lord is to obey His commandments.

Success is a constantly changing idea in cultures. In China, success could have been having the tiniest feet. In another culture it could have been to become a duchess. In some areas of America, a successful female is one who has made it up the corporate ladder. In another it is "being true to one's self."

But God's word never fails and the only time success was ever mentioned, it tells the whole story and it is the same solution given over and over throughout Scripture.

Be a good steward of your success and obey God's word.

9This course, "The Easiest Guide Ever to Stepping Out On Your Own" will be available in summer 2020 at www.truthandsong.com.

Week Nineteen / Day One: Gifts from God

Matthew 25:14-30

God gives us many things, but this week I am going to talk about six: spiritual gifts, our bodies, "talents," our mind, children and the fruit of our labor.

I guess when we traditionally think about talents, we might think of someone who can play sports well, sing professionally or is a genius in mathematics or science.

While those things are talents indeed, they aren't typical of the average person.

And to be honest, most people who are "gifted" find that it still takes time and practice to excel. There are quite a few studies that show how many hours people have invested in their "talent" before they were deemed successful.

But I am going to sidestep that traditional viewpoint and define "talent" as a gift of God given to you to use for His glory and profit.

Week Nineteen / Day Two: Spiritual gifts

Romans 12:1-13

I guess I first really pondered "spiritual gifts" in college, because it was given to us as an assignment. The professor said, "What do you think your spiritual gift is?"

I honestly had no clue. I had always just been the church pianist, but "church pianist" wasn't on the list. And you know what? That's okay if you don't recognize any distinct area toward where you seem bent.

I honestly believe that if you remain faithful in church, that God will place opportunities in your path. As you walk through open doors you will find what seems to work and what really doesn't.

For me, I could sit for hours and listen to someone discuss their problems, and then as I do my chores I find myself analyzing their situation and then Biblical solutions present themselves. I earned my Master's Degree in Biblical Counseling, but as I look back at myself as a child, I remember doing the same exact thing. I just didn't recognize it for what it was until much later.

But I have never really been a "Martha." I would much rather have a pile of dishes awaiting me in the morning after a get-together than to stop fellowshipping to deal with the mess or ask someone to help me clean up. Over and over I find myself writing, listening, teaching and encouraging. I would label my gifts as "teaching and exhortation."

Still, if you would have asked me that ten years ago, I wouldn't have known. What I do know is this. I stayed faithful in church and serving where I could. Be a faithful steward and see God reveal your gifts.

Week Nineteen / Day Three: Our bodies

1 Corinthians 16:20

How many times have you heard the phrase, “Well, everybody is going to die sometime. So we might as well enjoy life now.”

I have heard it more than I want to and especially in regards to the stewardship of our bodies. My response is generally this, “I am not afraid of dying. I am afraid of spending 10 years on dialysis, or spending $3000 a month on prescriptions, or having a lesser quality of life because I am chronically ill due to my own poor choices.”

Now, I am not advocating extremism in any way. Let your moderation be known unto men. People can get caught up and spend way too much time and money involved in their own looks. I am talking about just taking care of the body God gave you.

We literally only have the one body, and yet how many Christians are gluttons? How many Christians do not get enough water and rest? How many mock eating naturally and are taking blood pressure medication in their 30’s?

Start making good habits when you are young, because those seeds you sow in your 20’s usually come to fruition in your early 40’s and they are not always reversible.

Don’t limit your service to the Lord because you abused the temple of the Lord. Be a good steward of your health.

Week Nineteen / Day Four: “Talents”

Matthew 25:14-30

I have never really been the best at anything. My husband and I laugh because our family motto is “work really hard for mediocrity.” I wasn’t the smartest kid in school or college. I know many musicians who just seem to run their fingers up and down the piano and land on the right note every time: not me. While I can make money, it seems that I am destined as an educator to be involved in sales of my products and I am lousy at sales.

To be honest, it seemed that the other girls were always getting the boyfriends and I seemed to be invisible (although I did date a lot, but I am sure it was me compromising due to my heart’s desire for attention.)

I remember one time trying to sing harmony and someone responded, “What exactly are you trying to sing?” Ouch. But I try. I really try. I used to sing for hours in my bedroom wishing I had one of those smooth alto voices, but I kept singing. Now I have produced several [10]CDs on which I sing the melody and harmony.

This year I am trying to learn how to arrange music on paper and create sheet music. I am just awful. Maybe as God sees that I am taking my two talents and trying to double them, He will help me along.

I would encourage you to keep learning, keep trying, keep growing and doing things that are uncomfortable (like writing a devotional is scary for me). Because looking back, even if you aren’t the best, you will have done far more than you ever would have done if you had just given up.

10These can be found at www.truthandsong.com, itunes, spotify and amazon.

Week Nineteen / Day Five: Mind

Mark 12:30, Luke 10:27, Romans 8:7, Romans 12:2, Philippians 2:3, 1 Thessalonians 5:14

Not everyone was gifted with a strong mind. We are told to comfort those who are of a feeble mind, and we are to love the Lord with all our mind.

But I want to talk today specifically about how you are renewing your mind. I have seen in recent years the effect of people who were once Biblically minded literally change their entire outlook on life.

I started analyzing what these people had in common. Because I study people, whenever I started noticing people's vocabulary changing about God I just started watching to see what else was changing.

The one common element in all of them was their music. The musicians they pumped into their ears for who knows how long each day "renewed their mind" according to the musicians outlook on life.

I think about one girl who was struggling with suicidal thoughts. In a few years, the lead singer of her favorite band committed suicide. Also, "Christian musicians" can be so very dangerously influential, because they can be self-deceived and be the blind leading the blind.

In a time of seducing spirits, be vigilant like Timothy to know if those who have your eargate merely "profess Christ." Know first and foremost their doctrine and manner of life, and consider where they are headed? Those who have your eargate have your mind. (2 Timothy 3:10-11, Hebrews 13:7)

Be a good steward and diligent to know if it is being renewed in truth or deceit.

Week Nineteen / Day Six: Children

Proverbs 22:6, Proverbs 27:23

The desires of our heart are a tricky thing. Sometimes it feels like we want something so badly we could just explode. Our mind literally doesn't rest because we keep thinking upon this great desire.

This is how it feels when you want a baby and yet each month time goes by so slowly until you find if your hopes are dashed and before they are then again renewed.

But then there are some who seem to have children so easily and they can view them as either a burden or a blessing.

One thing that cannot be denied is that if God gave you children they are something that is given to us specifically. You can raise them up for the Lord or you can neglect your duties and get distracted by other desires or securities.

We all can either take what we have already learned and teach the children so that they can begin their life with a greater advantage, or we can let the world, their peers and media teach them there is no God, morality is relative and success is loving yourself first.

I have never regretted the time I took to learn everything I could about child training. I consider devotions with my kids the most important part of my day in regards to their well being. I try to live my life as the very best Christian that I can be to show them in every way that Biblical Living is God's wisdom passed down to them for their good as well as His glory.

If God gives you children, be a diligent steward of them.

Week Nineteen / Day Seven: Fruits of your labor

Ecclesiastes 3:12, 5:19, Proverbs 24:30-34

Some people seem more prone than others to just live in the moment and enjoy all that God has given them. For me, I have to read these verses to remind myself that it is not God that is making me feel guilty for relaxing and doing nothing but enjoying the simple pleasures of life.

We are to be stewards of our time (and we'll talk about that next week), but whether you are a driven go-getter or a "you only live once" personality, you need to be moderate in the way you live.

What a blessing to sit back and enjoy the sunshine on our shoulders while relaxing in our favorite chair with our favorite coffee or tea. What a joy to enjoy the laughter of friends and family. What a pleasure to stop working at the end of the day and just recharge.

On the flip side, we have to be careful to not get in a rut and waste our time away.

That is what we will talk about tomorrow.

Week Twenty / Day One: Our priorities

Ephesians 5:15-17

What do you deem most valuable in your life?

Is it winning the lost? Pleasing the Lord? Being faithful to church? Marrying a good Christian man? Being independent financially? Staying debt free? Having good grades in school? Finding a ministry? Getting a degree? Finding a good job? Moving out of your home? Continually bettering yourself? Eating a healthy diet? Having better skin?

Those are all great options within certain guidelines.

But have you prayed about which of these priorities, which are all within the "non-sinning realm," should rank at the top?

Have you searched the Bible for God's opinion on them?

Then I would further encourage you to write them down in a list and rank them accordingly with God's emphasis and then your desires as well. Remember none of them are wrong within certain guidelines. This is not a trick assignment.

Finally, see how much emphasis you are putting in pursuing them with your time.

Week Twenty / Day Two: Our priorities

Matthew 6:33-34

There is so much I could say about time management and building good habits. We honestly become what we do every day.

For me my daily time priorities (which are built around church attendance) are these: 1) Devotions with kids and prayer time alone. 2) Have everything done to spend fun time with husband and kids after dinner. 3) Healthy food prep. 4) Homeschool and piano lessons for my children (during the school year). 5) Manage household chores. 6) Ministry / soul winning and 7) Learning.

My schedule reflects those priorities and I don't really get involved in much else. I have found for me that if I add one more thing into the mix, something on my top seven stops getting done.

I have found that if I put ministry before anything else, it can become all consuming and a few other things that are greater in priority stop getting done.

I would encourage you to look at your list that you made yesterday and write out your own routine. Yours might be completely different from mine, but a list will you give you a starting point for how you can start making your priorities a reality.

Week Twenty / Day Three: Diligence

Proverbs 12:24, Proverbs 12:27, Proverbs 18:9, Matthew 25:26, Romans 12:11, Hebrews 6:12

I do love to dream and plan, but the hardest part of planning is the follow through. I have bought vegetables for the week and thrown them out because I didn't prepare them and they rotted. I try very hard to not thaw meat before I know I will cook it so that I don't waste God's provision.

I have written out savings plans and budgets, exercise regimes (think of the typical New Year's Resolutions) and then felt discouraged as I didn't stick to them.

But over the past ten years I have learned some things. I try to be very realistic about who I am and what I already am doing. When it comes to spending money, we look at how much it costs to live (without the extras) and then we work our hardest to make that much and not be careless or frivolous. The diligence aspect comes in when with every paycheck, we go through our expenses and make sure we are staying on track.

That is one way we use our time diligently. It would be easier to bury our head in the sand and not look, but there must be a day to give an account of our actions or our goals will not be accomplished.

The same things goes with food preparation. I look at how much time I have to make food and then I figure out ways to make healthy choices within that. When I go grocery shopping I only buy what I know I will cook and eat. Then I just try to be faithful and not wasteful.

What goals could you accomplish realistically by just adding diligence?

Week Twenty / Day Four: Diligence

Luke 16:1-13, 1 Timothy 6:6-12

Let's look a little more about diligence. Between 18 - 30 years of age there are a lot of choices and changes and it seems that looking ahead for that next thing becomes a major part of who we are.

"Life will really begin when I get married." or "Now that we are married, when will we have our first child?" and then, "I can't wait until our child starts school," and so on.

But to be honest, there is a lot of time between big life changing events. A lot of life is just routine maintenance. If you ask someone what they have been up to, very often the answer will be "work."

It can be tempting to become discontented and bored with just living and making ends meet, but if every day you spend time with the Lord and live to please Him, your faithfulness is pleasing to Him.

I read recently about Paul telling servants in bondage not to be angry at their masters, but to serve them with singleness of heart as unto the Lord. How can being a faithful servant with a good attitude be just as important as someone who seems to have the free time to be a soul winner each and every day?

That is why I do make my priority list and do my best to be faithful each day, because at the end of the day when the fiery darts cry, "What's the point?" I respond with, "Was I faithful in the little things?" and sleep in peace.

Week Twenty / Day Five: Church attendance

1 Timothy 3:15, Hebrews 10:25, Luke 4:16

I mentioned at the beginning of the week how I build my priorities around church attendance.

I honestly don't believe you can be a faithful steward of your time and miss church regularly. Even Jesus made it his custom weekly to go to the temple for the reading of the Scriptures, and he was perfect.

It doesn't matter how much I read the Bible or pray, nothing replaces the "foolishness of preaching." No amount of awe of God's creation and our own private worship changes the fact that God spent a large part of the New Testament talking specifically to churches about the order of the church.

Organized religion cannot be ignored if you are a student of the Scriptures. God called the church the pillar and ground of the truth. If the Bible is our foundation, the church is the support beam. Without that pillar our life will start to crack and crumble and becomes hazardous.

What I appreciate is God's emphasis that not only are we not to forsake the assembling, but also do gather "so much the more, as ye see the day approaching." *(I am assuming here that you already attend a sound, Bible-preaching church.)*

I would encourage you to trust God with your time and put Him first in every way.

Week Twenty / Day Six: Ministry and soul winning

Proverbs 11:30

I remember going to Bible college and struggling to fill out the weekly "Christian ministries" report. It required a certain amount of soul winning and church ministry and I just did not do well.

I went to class from 8 - 12, then practiced with their travelling music group from 1 - 2. I headed to work around 3 and did the closing shift. After work I did homework, devotions and headed to bed. I worked on Saturdays and did my laundry and chores then as well.

Today my schedule feels similar. I have never really been great at "door-to-door soul winning." But what I have tried to do is hand out tracts to every person I meet. If I casually talk to someone regularly I try to bring up Christ. A few times a year our family walks through our neighborhood and puts tracts and a John and Romans booklet on each door.

I am homebound because of health reasons and I do this ministry a couple of hours each day from home. I do what I can while still making sure that I am first and foremost honourable in being a keeper and guide at home.

This is an area that takes purposeful effort to accomplish, because life in general takes so much time and energy.

I don't know your commitments, but I would encourage you to look at your life and see what you *can do* and then purposefully prepare to minister to others and speak up for Christ every opportunity you can.

Week Twenty / Day Seven: Time with God

Proverbs 15:8, Matthew 6:21-34, Matthew 22:36-40

Out of everything this devotional accomplishes, I pray that it will cause you to want to regularly spend time with the Lord in prayer, Bible reading and Bible studying.

First build your routine around church and then place your devotional life as the next non-moving priority.

I promise that everything else will work itself into place if you can make those two things your main goals. Money comes and money goes, but your friendship with the Lord satisfies like nothing else.

You can spend all your time and give your best to your employer and then they don't recognize your hard work. God is not unrighteous to forget your work and labor of love.

You can give you heart and time away to someone but when you find yourself lonely despite all the people around you, God is the balm that heals the heart.

Let me leave you with these last thoughts. You can trust Him. Give Him your very best of you.

Now that I have covered "Why We Believe What We Believe" about things *within* the Bible, now I want to cover why we can trust the Bible.

Part Five

Why Can We Trust The Bible?

I was recently reading up on some works by a well-known atheist and he spent nearly 400 pages giving his viewpoint on why there is no God, no *real* scientist that actually believes creation, that science and creation cannot co-exist, and why religion persists even though it is not necessary for "survival."

He said that the Bible contradicts itself. That there is no real evidence to support that Jesus existed. That prophecies were manufactured much like horoscopes - vaguely and for the gullible and that most of the world's evils were done in the name of religion.

Do you know the "why" behind "what" you believe?

Can you answer why we believe Jesus was born in Bethlehem? Or why evolution isn't possible and creation is? Or why the Bible is a legitimate historical document and why it wasn't all written in 150 A.D.? In six weeks you will!

I know that a lot of these next six weeks are not going to be touchy- feely or "spiritual," but I assure you, they have everything to do with the Bible. The Bible is truth: scientific, historical, prophetic, practical and spiritual.

These are the issues that will be attacked strongly as you head into college, the workforce and as you try to witness to our increasingly atheistic culture. Try to glean as much as you can as you strengthen your faith in truth.

NOTE: If this any part of this section is too technical, feel free to skim over the details, grasp the idea and know that it is here to help you in a time of need.

Week Twenty-One / Day One: Where does intelligent life begin?

Psalm 90:1-2, Revelation 1:8, 4:8 & 10:5-6

One question that both creationists and evolutionists have to answer is "Where did intelligent life begin?"

The creationists say that God always was, is and will be, and that while we do not understand how God can exist outside of time and energy, we can see that someone must. **Why must someone have lived outside time and energy as we know it? Because of the laws of science.**

The first law of Thermodynamics tells us that energy can never be created or destroyed. They can only change from one kind of energy to another. The total amount of energy and matter in the universe is already set. We can't add to it, and we can't take away from it.[11]

Someone explained it like this. There is a painting and there is a painter. The painter exists outside of the painting. They set the canvas size, the paint color and the final outcome, but the painter itself is not bound by those rules, the finished painting is.

God planned how His creation (our universe) would run and gave it a beginning and an end. He created a certain amount of energy and a cycle by which it renews, but He is not bound by those rules outside of the universe.

But evolution's best minds cannot come up with a scientific solution to the same question of how there is energy if "energy cannot be created or destroyed."

11Apologia, "Exploring Creation with Chemistry and Physics" p. 184

Week Twenty-One / Day Two: Where does intelligent life begin?

1 Timothy 6:19-21, Colossians 1:16-20, John 1:3

In the video "Unlocking the Mysteries of Life" the leading chemical evolutionists were stumped by a question from a student. The question was given, "What was the source of the biological information in DNA?"

Ray Comfort's "The Athiest Delusion" (2016) asks the same question to scientists.

(Both of these videos can be found on Youtube and they give you an entertaining and scientific overlook of why this is the question that all scientists need to answer and why it can't be found in evolution)

The basic premise is this:

Fact: DNA contains all the instructions needed to build any form of life and the self-replication to sustain it.

Question: How could such writing come about without a writer, such programming without a programmer?

Would not those written instructions convince you that there must be some intelligent mind at work here? Does not writing require a writer?

If evolution can't answer the question of "Who wrote DNA?" then it would mean that there is another answer out there.

Week Twenty-One / Day Three: Design, natural selection and irreducible complexity.

Genesis 1:1-15

Have you ever hear of the term “Irreducible complexity?”

Irreducible complexity is just a fancy phrase to mean a single system which is composed of several interacting parts, and where the removal of any one of the parts causes the system to cease functioning. (Behe, 1996, speech delivered to the Discovery Institute) [12]

Because irreducible complexity has challenged evolutionist for years and the idea that survival of the fitest or adaptation to an environment is what causes the differences in living beings, they have countered the argument with a new idea: “accumulation.”

Richard Dawkins says, [13] “Chance is not a solution, given the high levels of improbability we see in living organisms, and no sane biologist ever suggested that it was. Design is not the real solution either.”

“Natural selection is a better alternative. Indeed, **design is not a real alternative at all because it raises an even bigger problem than it solves: who designed the designer?”** “The creationist completely misses the point, because ... he doesn’t understand accumulation.”

He concludes, “The creationists are right that, if genuine irreducible complexity could be properly demonstrated, it would wreck Darwin’s theory.” but that even Darwin said, “I can find no such case.”

12https://content.csbs.utah.edu/~rogers/evidevolcrs/ircomp/
13Richard Dawkins, The God Delusion, p. 145 - 146

Week Twenty-One / Day Four: Design, natural selection and irreducible complexity.

Genesis 1:16-31

Yesterday we read the evolutionist's presumption that there is no demonstrable case of irreducible complexity.

I again would encourage you to watch Unlocking The Mystery of Life to see how the "bacterial flagellar motor" is indeed irreducibly complex. (It can be watched on Youtube or purchased inexpensively.)

But I want you to also think about the evolutiont's idea of "accumulation."

They now believe that natural selection is conscious and intentional about storing stagnant and useless parts for the future.[14]

This poses two problems:

1. From where did this intelligent consciousness come?
2. If the laws of science say that everything naturally declines into disorder (entropy), how can natural selection be true?

14Richard Dawkins, The God Delusion, p. 245, p. 212, p. 141

Week Twenty-One / Day Five: God created intelligent life

Genesis 2

The question always comes back to origin.

Athiests ask, “Who designed the designer?”

Creationists ask, “From where did intelligence and consciousness come?

I don't believe there is an answer outside of Scripture, but evolutionists are still hoping to find one.

What I do hope to show you is this. we can believe there is a Creator even though we can't understand how He exists.

How? We can intelligently conclude that the Bible is trustworthy.

Week Twenty-One / Day Six: The origins of sin

Genesis 3, Romans 13

One thing that is the focus of the majority of the "God Delusion" is the idea that religion is a genetic deformity, and that it is passed from generation to generation or people group to people group.

If you don't understand church history and you don't discern between one group who claims "Christianity" and another, it does seem that a lot of evil is done in the name of "God."

But the Crusades were the Muslims and Catholics fighting for "the kingdom." The Dark Ages were Catholics killing anyone who dared speak against the church / state (pagan or Bible believer or scientist alike.)

Nero was a pagan who persecuted the New Testament church.

But in recent history persecution was heavy upon the Separatists, Waldensians, Ana-Baptists and Moldovans. Still, they were the ones promoting freedom of religion everywhere they went.

It is in man's sin nature to lust over power and money and the one thing that is deemed dangerous to those seeking control is people who believe in a Higher Power than man.

I guess in that sense, religion in all forms has been manipulated to cause many evils, but Bible believers in general are told to obey their authorities, pray for them and allow freedom of conscience.

Week Twenty-One / Day Seven: The purpose of the flood

Genesis 4-6:1-8

One accusation the gets thrown at those who believe in the God of the Bible is based around the flood. The claim comes in two fold. 1). If religion was any good, than it would make good people who weren't violent and 2). God committed genocide and is sadistic and bloodthirsty.

As a Bible-believer, I look at the flood in a completely different way. I see that man has a sin nature and the devil is the prince and power of the air. The devil is bloodthirsty and evil and so are those who follow him (religious or not).

God on the other hand gave men over 100 years to repent of their evil as Noah built the ark and preached for people to believe.

It was man who rejected salvation time and time again. It was mankind who refused to listen to their conscience as violence covered the earth. It was God who in His long-suffering ways gave them time to be saved.

And it was God who caused a world-wide event that gave us a whole other level of scientific evidence to support Scripture. We will look at that next week.

I hope this week has helped you to see that the origins of life, the laws of science and the origins of intelligence all work hand in hand with creation, and yet evolution still cannot come up with workable evidence to support the chemical origins of life or intelligence of matter.

Week Twenty-Two / Day One: The flood legends

Genesis 6:9-22, 11:1-9

It isn't just science that gives observable evidence of a creator. History as God describes it in the Bible has also been confirmed in secular cultures. The flood is one of those historical moments.

[15]Dr. Duane Gish, in Dinosaurs by Design, says there are more than 270 stories from different cultures around the world about a devastating flood.

Hawaiians have a flood story that tells of a time when, long after the death of the first man, the world became a wicked, terrible place. Only one good man was left, and his name was Nu-u. He made a great canoe with a house on it and filled it with animals. In this story, the waters came up over all the earth and killed all the people, only Nu-u and his family were saved.

Another flood story is from China. It records that Guhi, his wife, three sons, and three daughters escaped a great flood and were the only people alive on earth. After the great flood, the repopulated the world."

In fact, it has been shown that the ancient chinese symbol for boat is made up of the symbols for "vessel," "eight" and "people."

If you looked up "flood legends" you would see how many people groups passed down the story of the flood (presumably after they dispersed from the tower of babel) as they developed into indigenous cultures. But science also points to a worldwide flood.

15AnswersInGenesis.org

Week Twenty-Two / Day Two: The fossil evidence

Genesis 7

It is a common evolutionary idea that fossils give "prehistoric" evidence of our human evolution. Whenever I see the word "prehistoric," I literally think, "pre-flood" because historic evidence of intelligent life begins about 2300 B.C. in the "Fertile Crescent." The Greeks refer to this area as "Mesopotamia" which means "land between the rivers." Others call this spot the "Cradle of Civilization" because signs of early man exist there. These terms all refer to the same area in Iraq.

Mount Ararat, the mountain where Noah's ark landed, is just north of the Fertile Crescent between the Caspian and Black Seas.

That being said, fossils are our major wealth of "prehistoric" knowledge of life. They are part of historical science. This means that the creation of these fossils can't be tested, observed and repeated to conclude a specific fact or date (observable science). Historical science rather is subjective and involves the *interpretation* of evidence and the deduction of past occurrences.

With that in mind what we can see is that rapid, catastrophic burial does explain the geological features of many fossils.[16] Let's look at those tomorrow.

16www.AnswersInGenesis.org

Week Twenty-Two / Day Three: The fossil evidence

Genesis 8:1-14

I remember a presentation in church was given on geological evidence of the flood. When I saw the fossils of many types of animals extending their head in a common position known to be caused by suffocation, and it made my heart sink in compassion for the animals. There were so many fossils of animals with their head arched back as if in pain or gasping for air for it to be a coincidence.

In an article in N.Y. Times, it speaks of this phenomenon called "opisthotonus." They say, "To fossilize in the traumatic death position, a carcass would have to be quickly buried in the exact spot it died, without any transportation."

Another scientist who wanted to disprove a quick burial said that if the animals had died in water, it could account for their neck muscles bending backward and then their fossils being buried over time.

Both of their conclusions coincide with a flood.

Then there are the fossils of: Reptiles giving birth, [17]preservation of soft parts and creatures like jellyfish that have no hard parts, and if I had the time I could share so many more.

It is hard to deny that the fossil evidence points to the flood, but the flood isn't the only historical point of the Bible that has been confirmed by tangible evidence.

17www.AnswersInGenesis.org

Week Twenty-Two / Day Three: A privileged planet

Romans 1:18-22

Why did God say that man is without excuse? It was because the invisible (the spiritual things) are clearly seen in creation. God placed Earth in a specific spot in our solar system so that we could look out and see the universe. Did you know that? He wants us to see how He does things and His "eternal power."

Even secular sources know that Earth is one special planet. It is called the "Goldilocks planet." [18]"Though other bodies in our solar system, such as Saturn's moon Titan, seem like they could have once been hospitable to some form of life, and scientists still have hope of eventually digging up microbes beneath the surface of Mars, Earth is still the only world known to support life."

"The fact that Earth hosts not just life, but intelligent life, makes it doubly unique." *(Keep in mind, it is this issue of intelligent life that cannot be explained by evolutionists.)*

But even if living matter never became "intelligent," how is it that Earth is still the only planet that perfectly supports life? I want to answer those specifics in the next few days.

18www.space.com

Week Twenty-Two / Day Four: A water world

Proverbs 8

I love this chapter in the Bible. First of all, I love the character of "wisdom" in the Proverbs and how she tells all about herself. Wisdom is truth and truth is found in Scripture first and foremost. But here, she is talking about how she was the Lord's companion even before creation. (v.26 - 30)

But I also love this glimpse into creation. When there were no depths … no fountains abounding with water … when He established the clouds above … the fountains of the deep … when He gave to the sea His decree, that the waters should not pass His commandment .. when He set a compass upon the face of the depth. These all have to do with our planet being a water planet and the gravitational pull that keeps our waters exactly where they need to be.

Astronomer Geoffrey Marcy says, [19]"The most impressive attribute of the Earth is the existence and amount of liquid water on its surface." "The Earth is remarkable for its precisely-tuned amount of water, not too much to cover the mountains, and not so little that it's a dry desert, as Mars and Venus, our 'sister' planets."

"Earth's water is also special in that it has remained liquid for so long. How has Earth been able to hold on to its oceans while those on other planets freeze or fry?"

Those are tough questions for evolutionists, but easy for a creationist.

19www.space.com

Week Twenty-Two / Day Five: A "just right" location in the solar system

Psalm 19:1

Did you know that if the earth wasn't placed exactly where it is in our solar system, not only would it destroy its hospitality to life but we also would not be able to see the universe free from debris and gases? This is how God can say, "The heavens declare the glory of God" and know that it is declaring it to us.

The movie "The Privileged Planet" gives an excellent illustration of where we are located at a precise distance from the galaxy's center in a "co-rotation radius" that causes us to stay just where we are rather than being swept up in the spiral arms.

Our exact location puts us in a location that is safer than anywhere else in the universe. [20]"The presence of our big brother planet, Jupiter, farther out in the solar system … has helped Earth become a safe haven for life. Jupiter acts like a giant broom, sweeping the solar system of debris." [21] "We are removed from the more densely occupied areas, where stellar interactions can lead to disruption of planetary orbits. In addition, we are farther from the deadly affects of supernovae explosions." So we don't get bumped or burned to death.

But if the earth's gravitational pull was off by even the tiniest percentage, not only would we have already been destroyed, life would have never begun in the first place … let alone intelligent life. That is why the moon is so important. We will talk about that tomorrow.

20www.space.com
21http://godandscience.org/apologetics/designss.html

Week Twenty-Two / Day Five: A “friendly moon”

Psalm 8

“When I consider the heavens, the work of thy fingers, the moon and the stars” ... for ages the heavens have caused people groups all over the world to worship. They might not always know the God of the Bible, but they know there is something bigger than them. And the stars proclaim that.

But did you know that our moon is considered impossibly huge? Due to its large mass, scientists now know that it 1) could not have bulged off due to earth’s high rotational speed or 2) could not have been captured by the earth’s gravity.

Although evolutionists cannot explain the moon’s existence, they can see [22]that 1) the moon pulls the ocean’s tides (with the help of the sun), 2) stabilizes our planet’s rotation, preventing drastic movements of the poles that could cause massive changes in climate, and 3) keeps us in a 24 hour rotational cycle that keeps us from being thrown out into space at 500 miles per hour.

Don Brownlee, author of the book “Rare Earth” says, “I doubt that in our galaxy typical stars have planets just like Earth around them. I’m sure there are lots of planets in the galaxy that are somewhat similar to Earth, but the idea that this is a typical planet in nonsensical.”

Although, evolutionists claim that Earth is quite common, they have yet to find any evidence that supports their hopes.

22www.space.com

Week Twenty-Two / Day Six: A thin atmosphere and a metal core

Deuteronomy 4:14-19, Acts 14:6-14, Proverbs 8:27

God knew the heavens were so complex that people would worship them if they were not taught the truth. This is exactly what we find in Acts 14. But I want to point out another major difference between our surrounding planets and the earth.

We can breathe.

The earth is 20% more massive than Venus and further away from the sun. By all evolutionary[23] accounts our atmosphere would be thicker than that of Venus. But [24]"another 'just right' aspect of Earth is its size: If it was much smaller, it wouldn't be able to hold on to our precious atmosphere, but much larger and it might be a gas giant too hot for life."

But we also have a magnetic field, "a compass upon the face of the depth:". [25]"This magnetic field produces the Van-Allen radiation shield, which protects the Earth from radiation bombardment. If this shield were not present, life would not be possible on the Earth. The only other rocky planet to have any magnetic field is Mercury—but its field strength is 100 times less than the Earth's. Even Venus, our sister planet, has no magnetic field."

When Earth is "just right" it makes one wonder how in "billions of years" no other planet has done the same.

23www.godandscience.org
24www.space.com
25www.godandscience.org

Week Twenty-Two / Day Seven: Adding up the evidence

Ephesians 1:15-23

We can talk all the more about 1) plate tectonics that regulate that water's temperatures and water that lubricates the plate tectonics, 2) our exact axis tilt that sustains our 4 seasons, 3) an unusually circular orbit, and 4) the protective greenhouse effect of our gases that absorb and retain heat and block UV rays from the sun.

If any one of these things I have mentioned this week were not "just right" than life could not be sustained on earth.

I want to conclude these first two weeks by pointing out that there is plenty of scientific evidence to show the hand of a Creator. 1) The absolute energy of the entire universe must be explained due to the 1st Law of Thermodynamics, 2) The origins of DNA instructions and life itself, 3) The origins of intelligent life, 4) The 2nd Law of Thermodynamics is the opposite of natural selection, 5) A privileged planet that sustains and supports life, 6) Fossils that point to a worldwide flood and 7) Historical support of flood legends.

While the existence of a creator are still a mystery, we can still see much evidence for His existence. But science is just one piece of the puzzle. Let's look at the historical verifications of Scripture.

Week Twenty-Three / Day One: Original manuscripts aren't necessary

Jeremiah 37 (especially 27-28)

Some question the validity of the Bible because we do not have the original manuscripts. Couldn't they have just been made up? Haven't they lost their authority? But God saw this issue and answered it long ago.

In Jeremiah we see that he wrote out a manuscript for the King and the King burnt it. And the Lord said, "Take thee again another roll, and write in it all the former words that were in the first roll, which Johoiakim the king of Judah hath burned."

God wasn't concerned with an original. He was concerned with the words. A copy was sufficient. And the Bible has more manuscript evidence than any other piece of historical literature.

This week I want to give you some snapshots about the history of the Bible and why the King James Version is not only God's word, but a valid historical source.

Week Twenty-Three / Day Two: The Old Testament

Deuteronomy 4:1-6

[26]"The Old Testament - the 39 books from Genesis to Malachi - was written over a period of approximately 1,150 years. Eventually, due to age and wear, all of the autographs wore out or were lost. Through manuscripts, God preserved His Word. Today a multitude of manuscripts of the Bible still exist. While some include large sections of the Bible, others consist of single books, or chapters. A number of manuscripts fall into the fragment category, consisting of broken off, detached, or incomplete portions - some of which are too insignificant to even count."

"For generations, the Jews discussed and debated which books were inspired and belonged in the Old Testament. Finally, in A.D. 90, the rabbis (Jewish leaders) came together in the Council of Jamnia" and agreed upon the canon of Scripture we have today.

They understood the importance of having an officially accepted list of books lest someone add to it and pervert God's word.

"Between A.D. 500 - 1000, the Old Testament was copied by scribes known as the Masoretes." "They served a significant role in preserving the Old Testament." These manuscripts are known as the Masoretic Text. Two texts exist which claim to be Masoretic: *The Ben Chayyim Masoretic Text* and *The Ben Asher Masoretic Text*.

This is important. Stick with me as we look at these tomorrow.

26James C. Kahler, A Charted History of the Bible, p.6, 10

Week Twenty-Three / Day Three: The Old Testament

Psalm 109:6, Isaiah 14:12, 2 Peter 1:19, Revelation 22:16

The *Ben Asher Masoretic Text* was produced in the early 900's (A.D.). It "has been used to form present-day Hebrew texts," One of these is the *Biblia Hebraica* which has made [27]"over 20,000 changes to the traditional Masoretic Text. Most of the modern versions use one of the editions of *Biblia Hebraica* for the Old Testament for their Bibles."

Two of the most significant changes are 1) when they delete Satan's name in Psalm 109:6 and 2) where the word Lucifer is replaced with morning star or day star in Isaiah 14:12. As Jesus is the morning star and the daystar, this is a significant error.

"In 1516, a man by the name of Daniel Bomberg took the reliable Masoretic manuscripts, compiled them, and published a Hebrew text of the Old Testament referred to as the First Rabinnic Bible.

"The First Rabbinic Bible was followed in 1524-25 by a second edition completed by a Jewish rabbi named Jacob Ben Chayyim." *The Ben Chayyim Masoretic Text* is the Hebrew text from which the Old Testament of the King James Version was translated. "The majority of Masoretic Text manuscripts support it, and it alone can attest to being the faithful text of the Old Testament."

So, keep that in mind. There are two different texts which form two different lines of Bibles: the King James and the modern versions of the Old Testament.

27James C. Kahler, A Charted History of the Bible, p.10

Week Twenty-Three / Day Three: The Antiochan New Testament

Acts 11:25-27

[28]"The New Testament - the 27 books from Matthew to revelation - was completed by A.D. 95." "The New Testament was copied by hand by the early Church. In the first two centuries (A.D.), two major copying centers were producing manuscripts of the Bible. The copies coming from these two locations were very different and formed two streams of Bibles."

The first stream was the manuscripts from Antioch, Syria. [29]"After Jerusalem was destroyed in A.D. 70, Antioch became the center for Christian evangelism. With a vital emphasis on a historical-literal interpretation of Scripture, Antioch also naturally became a center for the preservation of the Bible."

95% of all known New Testament manuscripts fall into the Antioch stream. The Antioch manuscripts were compiled and in 1516 Desiderius Erasmus produced a Greek New Testament. (In 1598 its 5th edition became the basis for our English King James Bible)[30] and Tyndale translated an English New Testament in 1525.

These manuscripts go by other names: The Traditional Text, Byzantine Text, Imperial Text, Majority Text, Reformation Text, Syrain Text, and Universal Text. Over 5,500 manuscripts and the broad evidence of history (the acceptance of this text by the Christians) support the traditional text.[31]

28James C. Kahler, A Charted History of the Bible, p.12
29James C. Kahler, A Charted History of the Bible, p.15
30Samuel C. Gipp, Gipp's Understandable History of the Bible, Third Edition, p.113
31James C. Kahler, A Charted History of the Bible, p.15

Week Twenty-Three / Day Three: The Alexandrian New Testament

Acts 6:9, Acts 18:24-28

Biblically, Alexandria and Egypt have mostly been presented in a negative light. Alexandria was a hub of false doctrine and philosophy. The Alexandrian texts proceed from here. They are called the "minority texts" because out of the over 5,500 manuscripts that have survived, fewer than 50 are Alexandrian and some were found in the trash.

In 200, Origen (remember his name for later in regards to Josephus) became the leader of a school in Alexandria. Origen is the father of all Bible critics. He preferred to interpret the Bible allegorically rather than literally because he said some passages were impossible to read literally. He said, [32]*"Now what man of intelligence will believe that the first and the second and the third day ... existed without the sun and moon and stars?"*

[33]"It was this philosophy about Scripture that slanted all of the Alexandrian manuscripts. The Vaticanus and the Sinaiticus are the two most prominent manuscripts used as the basis for many of the new versions of the Bible. Although both come from Alexandria, these two manuscripts differ with one another around 70% of the time."

The Vaticanus Manuscript is property of the Roman Catholic Church. The Sinaiticus Manuscript was literally found in the trash molding and waiting to be burned, but they were "rescued" and reworked by as many as ten different writers. In spite of their errors, origins, and the minority of their texts they became the basis for our modern English New Testaments.

32www.christianitytoday.com
33James C. Kahler, A Charted History of the Bible, p.19

Week Twenty-Three / Day Four: The Seven English Bibles

Psalm 12:6-7

It is interesting that God not only said that he would keep his words and preserve them from this generation for ever, but that he also said he would purify them. Why would God need to purify them if they were already perfect? I think this points to the English texts of the Old and New Testaments.

[34]"When England - under Henry VIII - broke away from the Roman Catholic Church (1534), the way for English Bibles was finally paved!"

1) Coverdale's Bible (1535), 2) Matthew's Bible (1537), 3) Taverner's Bible (1539), 4) Great Bible (1539), 5) Geneva Bible (1557), 6) Bishop's Bible (1568) and 7) King James Version (1611).

The "modern English versions" take their New Testament from the Alexandrian minority manuscripts and most use the *Biblia Hebraica* for the Old Testament (both which change important word and remove doctrinal passages).

The English versions used largely the *Ben Chayyim Masoretic Text* for their Old Testament and the Antiochan Manuscripts for their New Testament.

These were good Bibles, some better than others, with the King James Version being the best. Let's look a little bit about why.

34James C. Kahler, A Charted History of the Bible, p.25

Week Twenty-Three / Day Five: The King James Translators

Psalm 119:140

One of the fascinating parts of the King James Bible is its story.

[35]"In 1604, a Puritan scholar named Dr. John Reynolds suggested to King James 1 of England that a new translation of the Bible was needed. The king agreed and fifty-four men - representing the finest Biblical scholarship - were appointed to the task. They were divided into six companies, each company with a center for meeting and a specific section of Scripture to translate."

[36]"The plan went like this: In each of the six companies, each member would work on a chapter or chapters individually. Then he would meet with his colleagues so that the whole company might debate the merits of any translation ...and come to a consensus of what should go in the final manuscripts."

In regards to the translators [37]"All were members of the Church of England, but their religious views ran the gamut. Some were ardent Puritans, others staunch defenders of the religious establishment. Some believed in pre-destination and limited salvation as taught by John Calvin, while others believed in self-determination and universal access to heaven as taught by Jacobus Arminius."

This caused them to naturally hold each other accountable, because no one wanted the other to put in their slant. Their diversity was part of what created a pure version.

35James C. Kahler, A Charted History of the Bible, p.10
36John Stevens Kerr, Ancient Texts Alive Today: The Story of the English Bible, p.115, 116
37https://kingjamesbibletranslators.org/bios/

Week Twenty-Three / Day Six: The English Language

Hebrews 4:12

When the Jews received the Old Testament, God gave them the Bible in their common language: Hebrew. When the gospel was presented to the whole world (Jews and Gentiles alike), God gave the Bible in Greek, the common language of the day. After the Reformation and just as the New World was being founded, God gave the world a Bible in their common language: English.

It is said that the King James Version changed the way the world speaks. In an article on that exact topic, a secular source says, [38]"Perhaps the most intriguing reason for the impact of the King James Bible is that it ignored what today would be essentials for good translation.

The translators seem to have taken the view that the best translation was a literal one, so instead of adapting Hebrew and Greek to English forms of speaking they simply translated it literally."

The King James Version [39]"rivaled its predecessors in simplicity and literary excellence, but the greatest improvement was the text itself. The translators had a better grasp and understanding of the original languages (Hebrew and Greek), enabling them to produce a Bible that was a faithful and more accurate translation of the very words inspired by the Holy Ghost."

Is it any wonder that your King James Bible is a living book that pierces even to the dividing asunder of the soul and spirit?

38www.bbc.com
39James C. Kahler, A Charted History of the Bible, p.16

Week Twenty-Three / Day Seven: The Bible is a historical document

1 Peter 1:25

The bibliographical test of a piece of historical literature examines how long the time interval was between the originals and the existing manuscripts and how consistent they are with each other as a group.

We have already seen that the Antiocan texts have over 5,500 texts that are in agreement with each other and the Ben Chayyim Masoratic Texts came from the earlier Masoretic Texts (500 - 1000 A.D.) and those are supported even further by the Dead Sea Scrolls (150 B.C.)

[40]This far surpasses The *Illiad* which is second in manuscript authority with 643 copies. And yet no one would dare question its authenticity, or that of *The History of Thucydides* (460-400 B.C.) whose manuscripts are scarce.

The Bible passes the standard bibliographic tests applied for ancient literature. It passes the scientific tests in regards to the creation account. Now let's move on to see how it passes the external evidence test: the Bible being compared to secular historical and archaeological accounts.

40Josh McDowell, More Than A Carpenter, p. 47, 48

Week Twenty-Four / Day One: Archaeological evidence

Ezekiel 28

This week is a bit harder for me to organize because archaeological evidence doesn't just answer one question. It tries to answer three: 1) Is the Bible historically reliable? 2) Was the Bible written when the authors claim or in the 2nd century A.D. like the skeptics accuse? and 3) Is there any evidence that it is divine?

As I tried to gather all of this evidence, I found that at every turn there was someone who would say, "That didn't really happen that way, because ..." and then would just give their opinion without any contrary evidence to support their viewpoint. Keep that in mind: evidence matters, opinions don't.

In regards to a historical document, it must be assumed that the writers did not set out to deceive. The manuscript must be given the benefit of the doubt unless it can be discredited. This is the general view regarding historical literature.

Today's passage is a prophecy about the city of Tyre and every single part of this prophecy has been fulfilled and is documented by archaeology. If you want to delve into this, an in-depth study can be found in *Evidence that Demands a Verdict* (a faith saving book).

Each of these pieces of evidence is so important, because while none have been found to discredit the Bible's reliability, more and more continues being found that supports it.

We will see more examples in the next few days.

Week Twenty-Four / Day Two: Moses, Abraham and the Ebla Kingdom

Genesis 13-14:1,2

I don't know if you have ever thought about it much, but [41]Moses was alive around 1450 B.C., Abraham's was alive in 1877 B.C. and the flood was approximately in 2305 B.C. How did Moses, who penned the first five books of the Old Testament, have such specific details of what happened "prehistorically" and then for the 300 years after the flood?

How did Moses know that Abraham lived in Ur of the Chaldees a suburb of Sumeria? How did he know that while Abraham was alive there was a huge battle between two sets of king listed in Genesis 14:1-2?

For many years Genesis has been criticized. Many said that Moses didn't live in a time where laws and history were recorded and that the cities and battles he described were made up.

Yet in 1968 some tablets were uncovered of the [42]Ebla Kingdom (2300 - 2250 B.C.). They mentioned the goddess Ishtar, and their laws and customs were recorded (Noah was around this time). But also on the tablets, they recorded five "Cities of the Plain" in the exact order given in Genesis 14:2: Sodom, Gomorrah, Admah, Zeboiim and Zoar.

Moses had to have had God-given knowledge! Pretty neat, huh?

I love stuff like that.

41www.creation.com
42Josh McDowell, Evidence That Demands A Verdict, p. 68

Week Twenty-Four / Day Three: Joshua and the battle of Jericho

Joshua 6

For some reason whenever I pictured the battle of Jericho, I literally imagined "the walls came tumbling down" like it began to crumble and landed in low heaps on the ground. But that isn't what the Bible says at all. It says that it fell down flat (v. 20).

[43]"During the excavations of Jericho (1930-1936) Garstang found something so startling that a statement of what was found was prepared and signed by himself and two other members of the team. In reference to these findings Garstan says: 'As to the main fact, then, there remains no doubt: the walls fell outwards so completely that the attackers would be able to clamber up and over their ruins into the city.' Why so unusual? Because the walls of cities do not fall outwards, they fall inwards. And yet in Joshua 6:20 we read ' … the was fell down flat, so that the people went up into the city, every man straight before him, and they took the city.' The walls were made to fall outward."

Only God can do that. And another example of archaeology showing that the Bible is true.

43Josh McDowell, Evidence That Demands A Verdict, p. 69

Week Twenty-Four / Day Four: Did King David really exist?

1 Kings 22

It was said that there was no archaeological evidence for King David's monarchy. That was until 1993 at the site of Ten Dan in northern Israel when archaeologist Avrahan Biram found an inscription made by an Aramean king who mentions defeating the "king of Israel" as well as "the king of the house of David."[44]

The age of this "tel Dan stela fragment" on a 9th century B.C. stone corresponds with the timeline of King Jehoshaphat of Israel and King Ahab of Judah (the house of David) who fought together to gain control of Ramoth in Gilead and lost.

The fact that any secular king would not only mention the house of David but also that both the king of Israel and king of Judah went to battle together is pretty significant.

But one of my favorite evidences of the accuracy of the Bible happened nearly 500 years after this battle. It is of Alexander the Great. Many people say the Bible was written all at one time after Christ died. They do this to account for how Christ fulfilled the prophecies of the Messiah.

Yet, history shows that these prophecies were written well before Christ's birth because Alexander the Great decided not to conquer Jerusalem after the high priest showed Alexander his very own prophecy. Tomorrow I will share Josephus, the Jewish historian's record of that meeting.

44www.BiblicalArcheology.org

Week Twenty-Four / Day Five: Alexander the Great's prophecy fulfilled

Daniel 10:1, 11:2-3

[45]"About 180 years before Alexander the Great was born, the Prophet Daniel wrote his book. Daniel 10:1 states that he wrote it in the third year of the reign of Cyrus the Great, which historians agree was around 535 b.c. Josephus, the Jewish historian who lived in the first century a.d., said that when Alexander was just about to enter Jerusalem, the Jewish high priest at that time, Jaddua, met him on the outskirts of the city.

Jaddua led a procession of affluent resident of Jerusalem. They hoped to convince Alexander not to make Jerusalem the next city he destroyed. The sight gave Alexander pause. Josephus records that Alexander had had a dream of this high priest and took this as a sign from God. He entered the city peacefully. Once inside, Jaddua brough Alexander to the temple and showed him passages from the book of Daniel.

Josephus wrote about Alexander's reaction to Jaddua in *Antiquities of the Jews:* "And when the book of Daniel was showed him wherein Daniel declared that one of the Greeks should destroy the empire of the Persians, he supposed that himself was the person intended. And as he was then glad, he dismissed the multitude for the present, but the next day he called them to him, and bid them ask what favors they pleased of him, whereupon the high priest desired that they might enjoy the laws of their forefathers, and might pay no tribute on the seventh year. He granted all they desired.

And when they entreated him that he would permit the Jews in Babylon and Media to enjoy their own laws also, he willingly promised to do hereafter what they desired."

45www.TheTrumpet.com

Week Twenty-Four / Day Six: New Testament archaeology

Acts 19:23 - 31

It is hard to argue against the accuracy of the Old Testament because it was written over such a long time and has quite a few fulfilled prophecies (not Christ-related) and miracles (Jericho) that are unexplainable without God's hand involved.

But the New Testament was written in a relatively short period of time. It was all written after Christ's resurrection and before John died in 95 A.D.. Yet, critics claim that all of the Bible was written after 120 A.D. to create "false prophecies" and "false fulfillment of prophecies."

1) Is there anything to support the New Testament being written in the 1st century A.D.? 2) Why would that even matter? 3) Is there anything to support that the New Testament is divine?

Let me answer those questions.

1) Yes, and I will go over that tomorrow.
2) It matters because if it wasn't written between 28 A.D. and 95 A.D. then the Apostles were liars and nothing they said about Christ could be trusted.
3) If the Apostles were credible, intelligent witnesses then what they said (and died for) about Christ's ministry and resurrection from the dead proves the prophecies about the Messiah were fulfilled in Christ. That would show a divine stamp of approval on the texts.

Today's passage talks about a theater in Ephesus. The theater was excavated and can be seen today[46].

---

46 http://www.israeljerusalem.com/theater-of-ephesus.htm

Week Twenty-Four / Day Seven: Luke

Colossians 4:11-14, 2 Timothy 4:11, Acts 16:9-20

I never realized how important Luke was until I started researching the arguments against the Bible's accuracy, but Luke (the doctor) was extremely specific in listing genealogies, rulers, cities, and places. It makes it tricky because if you are specific you can be both proven right or proven wrong.

[47]"Sir William Ramsay is regarded as one of the greatest archaeologists ever to have lived. ... He believed that the Book of Acts was a product of the mid-second century" While researching Asia Minor "he was compelled to consider the writings of Luke. As a result he was forced to do a complete reversal of his beliefs due to the overwhelming evidence uncovered in his research."

Ramsay concluded, "In all matters of external fact the author of Acts is seen to have been minutely careful and accurate as only a contemporary can be."

Here, we find yet another skeptic of the Scriptures convinced by evidence. Luke was a writer and contemporary of Christ (died 28 A.D.) and Paul (whose ministry can be historically traced to before 66 A.D.) are our most solid evidence to the historical accuracy of the New Testament.

But that still doesn't answer the question of the deity of Christ and whether Jesus and the Apostles were mistaken. Next week we will talk about evidences of the spirit world and Christ's ministry.

47Josh McDowell, Evidence That Demands A Verdict, p. 70

Week Twenty-Five / Day One: Jesus and the spirit world

Mark 5:1-20

I have a friend, Lena. She is an Indian from South Africa and was raised Hindu. She gave me her testimony once and it was fascinating because many Americans do not come into contact with the spirit world as do many people from Africa and the islands around the Atlantic and Pacific.

She said that Hinduism was leaving her family discontented and spiritually empty. She began her journey to really delve deep into her religion and still came back feeling like it was all a lie.

At the same time, her neighbor (a Christian) was having marriage problems. The husband was not particularly a great man, but one day while at his house their living room curtains suddenly burst into flames and the man said, “In the name of Jesus Christ, I command you to leave this house.” The flames immediately disappeared and the curtains were in perfect condition with no trace of the incident.

Lena thought, “How can the spirits be commanded this way and who is Jesus Christ?” Some may say that this was a hallucination, but do several people see the same hallucination and without any hallucinogens?

The spirit world exists. There is evidence for this in abundance, and for which I have no more time to write. But I wanted to give this specific example to answer the question “Who is Jesus Christ?”

Week Twenty-Five / Day Two: Jesus in history

John 1:1-34

Without Jesus, where would we be? But some say that his existence can't be proven historically. (They do not give credence to his tomb.) But there are a few mentions of him in secular history, and while these secular sources are widely accepted, they are highly criticized whenever Jesus is mentioned. The works of Flavius Josephus are no exception.

The 3rd century version of what Josephus said as recorded by Eusebius is rejected because Origen (Do you remember him?) said that Josephus was never converted to Christianity and an unbelieving Jew would never call Jesus "the Christ."

And so a 10th century manuscript is used to support that while Josephus did not call Jesus "Christ," he was still a figure of history. Here is the 3rd century wording.

[48] *"Now there was about this time Jesus, a wise man, if it be lawful to call him a man. For he was a doer of wonderful works, a teacher of such men as receive the truth with pleasure. He drew over to him both many of the Jews, and many of the Gentiles.*

He was [the] Christ. And when Pilate, at the suggestion of the principal men among us, had condemned him to the cross,[7] those that loved him at the first did not forsake him. For he appeared to them alive again, the third day:[8] as the divine prophets had foretold these and ten thousand other wonderful things concerning him. And the tribe of Christians, so named from him, are not extinct at this day."

Good ol' Alexandria spreading seeds of doubt again about Christ. Regardless, this criticism has been latched onto by many atheists. But the story doesn't end there.

48Flavius Josephus, Antiquities of the Jews - Book XVIII, Ch 3.3

Week Twenty-Five / Day Three: Jesus in history

Matthew 13:55-56, Mark 6:3

That isn't the only time Jesus was mentioned. Josephus mentioned Jesus again in relation to His half-brother James' death.

[49]"So he assembled the sanhedrin of judges, and brought before them the brother of Jesus who was called Christ, whose name was James: and some others, [or, some of his companions.] And when he had formed an accusation against them as breakers of the law, he delivered them to be stoned."

[50]"He was also mentioned by Tacitus (*Annals* 15:44), Suetonius (*Claudius* 25), and Pliny the Younger (*Letter to Trajan*).

Because these sources are embarrassing to the critics, "they have provoked many attacks, especially the two Josephus instances" but they "prove conclusively that any denial of Jesus' historicity is maundering sensationalism by the uninformed and/or the dishonest." Paul Maier, Professor of Ancient History

This is some deep stuff. I hope you are hanging in there with me. Even if you are glazing over a little bit, I hope you know that this is a valuable resource to you when your faith is challenged.

49Flavius Josephus, Antiquities of the Jews - Book XX, Ch 9
50https://www.namb.net/apologetics-blog/josephus-and-jesus/

Week Twenty-Five / Day Four: Did any other "religious leaders" claim they would rise again?

John 2:18-22, Matthew 12:39-40, Matthew 16:21, Matthew 27:62-64, John 10:17-18

While many people concede that Jesus was a historical figure, what they do deny is that he was the Messiah, divine or that he rose from the grave.

Many Jews believe that the Old Testament is a divine book of God and yet they deny that Christ is the Messiah saying that he was not born in Bethlehem, nor of a virgin. Their views have evolved into Hassidic Jewry and the worship of Kabbalah while still holding onto their cultural traditions.

Some Jews (being disillusioned by no fulfillment of a Messiah) believe their ancestors were involved in a tribal cult and have become atheists while assimilating into their local cultures.

Could Jesus have been mistaken? Could he have believed he was God and misled people out of a sincere heart? I ask this, "Did any 'well meaning' man say he would die and rise again on the third day?"

There might be false religions that piggy-back off of Christianity and confidence in Christ, but none that profess something so bold as a bodily resurrection.

1) Mohammed never dared make claims of resurrection and writings about Mohammed were written several hundred years after his death and all from being passed down by word of mouth.

2) Buddha's path of enlightenment centered on finding on personal spiritual development and achieving nirvana. Yet, no provable claims were made.

3) Hinduism is a spiritual religion with no one deity and certainly no prophecies or claims that could be seen or fulfilled.

Week Twenty-Five / Day Five: The empty tomb

Mark 16, 1 Corinthians 15

The empty tomb is one of the hallmarks of our faith. Many have died for their beliefs, but no other beliefs have an empty grave to prove their Savior lives.

The fact that there is an empty tomb tries to be "explained away" but it is a grave you can visit. The Gospel Coalition says this,

[51]"Why would the Jews circulate the story of Jesus's body being stolen by the disciples if the tomb was not empty? Why would the author of the Gospel of Matthew say that this lie was circulating if he knew that Jesus's tomb was not empty?"

In the second century, Justin Martyr recorded that this story was still being circulated in his day: "His disciples stole him by night from the tomb, where he was laid when unfastened from the cross, and now deceive men by asserting that he has risen from the dead and ascended to heaven" (*Diaolgue with Trypho*). Tertullian, in 200, also corroborated this idea: "This is he whom his disciples secretly stole away, that it might be said he had risen again, or the gardener abstracted, that his lettuces might come to no harm from the crowds of visitants!" (*De Spectaculis*).

Thus, there would be no need to propagate the idea that the disciples stole Jesus's body from the tomb if the tomb were not empty!"

This is just another evidence in the legal-historical proof of the Bible's accuracy, but the one I want to share tomorrow is kind of funny to me.

51https://www.thegospelcoalition.org/article/4-reasons-to-believe-in-the-empty-tomb/

Week Twenty-Five / Day Six: The empty tomb

Matthew 28

One of the reasons to believe the Bible's account of the resurrection of Christ is simply that if someone was going to "plan" a witness in those times, they certainly wouldn't use a woman to do it.

The Gospel Coalition explains:

[52]"Women were not considered credible witnesses. They were seen as being intellectually and morally deficient. Why, then, did the Gospel writers designate women as the first witnesses to the empty tomb and the risen Jesus? If the Gospel writers wanted to substantiate their message, they could have listed Peter and John or some other prominent disciples as the first witness. Surely any of the disciples would have been a better pick than these women! Why did they choose to include women as being the first witnesses? Because they were intent on recounting the story as truthfully as possible.

Embarrassment is one standard that historians use to gauge the historicity of a recorded event. If an author chooses to include an embarrassing fact that may hurt his/her case, then it is unlikely that he is making up his story. The fact that the Gospel writers included the "embarrassing" details of the women being the witnesses to the empty tomb shows the unlikelihood of the empty tomb narratives being fabricated."

We can believe the Bible because they were willing to tell the truth at their own expense.

This is the end of my study on the external evidence that supports Scripture. I want to go into the internal evidence and the impossibility that the authors of the Bible could prophecy about Christ and it be fulfilled hundreds of years later.

52https://www.thegospelcoalition.org/article/4-reasons-to-believe-in-the-empty-tomb/

Week Twenty-Five / Day Seven: Jesus declares He is equal with God

John 1:1 & 14, 8:19 & 58, 10:30, 12:45, 15:23

Let's do a quick recap: 1) Jesus said he would die and rise again on the third day, 2) His disciples said they and others were eyewitnesses of his resurrection, 3) There is historical evidence that there were people trying to explain away the empty tomb, and 4) Jesus claimed to be God.

But for Jesus to be God, he had to fulfill some pretty specific prophecies. They were indeed fulfilled! And there are some hard to understand "contradictions" between Scripture and history if you have never studied them before. I will explain all this next week, but here are the accusations.

1) THE TIMELINE OF JESUS'S BIRTH: Jesus could not have been born in Bethlehem because there was no census listed in history of a worldwide tax when Herod was alive (Matthew 2) and he died in 4 B.C.. Cyrenius did not become governor of Syria until 6 A.D. There is a 10 year gap. Matthew and Luke got it wrong somewhere.
2) THE SLAUGHTER OF THE INNOCENTS: If Herod really killed all the babies 2 and under across all the coasts (Matthew 2:16) wouldn't there have been a record of it?
3) THE GENEALOGIES DON'T MATCH: Not only do the genealogies contradict each other after they mention David, but they are both of Joseph. Jesus wasn't Joseph's son.

While I can't give proof that what I will explain happened exactly as I describe, given the Bible's history of accuracy, these are very possible explanations. There is no need for any reason to doubt their accuracy outside of a prejudice against Scripture.

Week Twenty-Six / Day One: The prophecies concerning Jesus fulfilled

The next few days, the passages I want you to look up are the prophecies and their fulfillments by Christ[53].

Jesus's betrayal by Judas, his friend

Prophecy (1000 B.C) Psalm 41:9

Fulfillment (31 A.D.) Matthew 26:47-50

30 pieces of silver

Prophecy (Between 520-518 B.C.) Zechariah 11:12-13

Fulfilled (About 28 A.D.) Matthew 26:15, 27:5-7

Jesus's back beaten, beard torn, face spit upon

Prophecy (700 - 681 B.C) Isaiah 50:6

Fulfillment (About 28 A.D.) Matthew 26:67, 27:26, Luke 22:63, 64,

Jesus silent before accusers

Prophecy (Between 701-681 BC) Isaiah 53:7

Fulfillment (About 28 A.D.) Matthew 27:12-14

Jesus to die for our sins

Prophecy (Between 701-681 BC) Isaiah 53:4-6

Fulfillment (About 28 A.D.) The gospels

Jesus numbered with the transgressors (thieves on the cross)

Prophecy (Between 701-681 BC) Isaiah 53:12

Fulfillment (About 28 A.D.) Mark 15:28

53100prophecies.org

Week Twenty-Six / Day Two: Prophecies of the specifics of Jesus's death

These are all about the details of Christ's crucifixion found in Psalm 22 (about 1000 B.C.) and their fulfilment (about 28 A.D.).

My God, My God, Why hast thou forsaken me?

Prophecy: Psalm 22:1

Fulfillment: Matthew 27:46, Mark 15:34

Scorn and shaking of the head

Prophecy : Psalm 22:7

Fulfillment: Matthew 27:31, 39, Mark 15:20, 29, Luke 22:63, 23:36

Mocking Jesus for the Lord to save Him

Prophecy: Psalm 22:8

Fulfillment: Matthew 27:43

Bones out of joint and heart bursting and pouring out water and blood

Prophecy: Psalm 22:14

Fulfillment: John 19:34

Feet and hands are pierced

Prophecy: Psalm 22:16

Fulfillment: John 19:23, 24, 37

Cast lots for his garments

Prophecy: Psalm 22:18

Fulfillment: Matthew 27:35

Week Twenty-Six / Day Three: The birth of Christ

Luke 2-3:23, Acts 5:37, Micah 5:2, Matthew 2:1-8

By using the Bible and the works of Josephus, here is a brief timeline of dates that are consistent with both scripture and history.

- 31 B.C. - Caesar Augustus defeated Antony
- 12 B.C. - Cyrenius becomes consul
- 6 B.C. - Grant Matthews "Star of Bethlehem" alignment of Jupiter, Saturn and Moon
- 5 B.C. - Jesus born (likely in the fall)
- 4 B.C. - Herod the Great dies (March / April)[54]
- 6 A.D. - A 2nd taxing mentioned in Acts. 5:36-37 [55]
- 10 A.D. - Herod the Tetrarch begins to reign[56]
- 25 A.D. - John the Baptist and Jesus begin their public ministry (Luke 3:1-23)

Let me point out what I discerned.

1) Luke did not "overlook" the local taxing in 6 A.D. He mentioned it in Acts 5:37 and gave specific details about Judas of Galilee which Josephus also mentioned. 2) A local tax is indeed different than a world wide tax and therefore this is not just a confusion, but something completely different. 3) Josephus did not say that Cyrenius was the governor of Syria in 6 A.D., but rather a [57]Roman senator. There is a difference and Josephus knew that. 4) The president of Syria was known to have governors ruling under him, and therefore, Cyrennius who "had gone through other magistracies" could have been governor of Syria in 5 B.C. under Quintilius Varus.

This study solidified my faith all the more, but now you have some facts in case anyone throws these accusations at you.

54Flavious Josephus, Antiquities of the Jews - Book XVII, Chapter 6
55Flavious Josephus, Antiquities of the Jews - Book XVIII, Chapter 1 & 2
56Flavious Josephus, Antiquities of the Jews - Book XVIII, Chapter 2
57Flavious Josephus, Antiquities of the Jews - Book XVII, Chapter 1

Week Twenty-Six / Day Four: The slaughter of the babies

Matthew 2, Jeremiah 31:15

One would think that if a ruler slaughtered all the children that were in Bethlehem, and in all the coasts thereof, from two years old and under, that it would make a huge mark in history.

There is not an exact record of that slaughter, because Herod was such a fearful king. But after Herod's death this is a portion of the appeal the Jews sent to Caesar asking him if they could become part of Syria and out of under a king.[58]

"They declared that he was indeed in name a King: but that he had taken to himself that uncontroulable authority which tyrants exercise over their subjects: and had made use of that authority for the destruction of the Jews: and did not abstain from making many innovations among them besides, according to his own inclinations. And that whereas there were a great many who perished by that destruction he brought upon them, so many indeed as no other history relates: they that survived were far more miserable than those that suffered under him, not only by the anxiety they were in from his looks and disposition towards them, but from the danger their estates were in of being taken away by him."

The first non-Christian reference to the massacre is recorded four centuries later by Macrobius (c. 395–423), who writes in his *Saturnalia*:

"When he [emperor Augustus] heard that among the boys in Syria under two years old whom Herod, king of the Jews, had ordered killed, his own son was also killed, he said: it is better to be Herod's pig, than his son."

Such a sad day. They suffered in silence.

58 Flavious Josephus, Antiquities of the Jews - Book XVII, Chapter 11

Week Twenty-Six / Day Five: Why do the genealogies contradict?

Read the prophecies and fulfillments and their Scriptures today

For Jesus to be the Messiah, he had to meet the following qualifications:

1) Jesus would be from Adam (Genesis 3:15, Luke 3:38)
2) Jesus would come from Judah / David (Genesis 49:10, Isaiah 11:1, Matthew 1:1-5, Luke 3:32-34)
3) Jesus could not be from the "seed of Jeconiah" (Jeremiah 22:30)
4) Jesus could not have a sin nature and must be born of a virgin. Because the sin is in the blood and the bloodline is passed through the males. (Isaiah 9:6-7, Romans 5:12)

To understand the family tree, you need to grasp a few things:

1) Why there are differences from David to Salathiel. (This is to fulfill the prophecy that Jeconiah's seed would not continue, but that he would still be in the "line" of Christ. Jeremiah 22:30.)
2) Neri was a "near kinsman" (Ruth 4:10) who raised up the name of the dead upon Jeconiah's inheritance through the line of Nathan (Solomon's older brother through Bathsheba) - 2 Samuel 5:14, 1 Chron. 3:5.
3) The pattern that Matthew and Luke are both skipping every other generation from Jeconiah / Neri through the grandsons of Zerubbabel: Abiud and Rhesa. This reconciles the differences after Zerubbabel. They are his grandsons.
4) Continuing the skipping of generations, we are safe to assume that Jacob and Heli are both Joseph's grandfathers.
5) Mary very likley shares Heli as a grandfather with Joseph. According to tradition (Numbers 36, Genesis 24 & Genesis 29)

Week Twenty-Six / Day Six: Jesus' family tree

Jeremiah 22:30, 1 Chronicles 3:15-19, Matthew 1, Luke 3:23-38

Adam to Abraham — Luke 3:35-38

Matt. 1:1-5 — **Abraham to David** — Luke 3:32-34

Josiah's Genealogy

1 Chron. 3 — * Solomon to Josias

Neri's Genealogy

Nathan to Neri — Luke 3:27-31

Zerubbabels Genealogy proven to not be of the "seed" of Jeconiah, but of Neri.

Jeconiah

Matt. 1:11 — Neri — Jer. 22:30 & Luke 3:27

Jeconiah's widow marries "near kinsman" Neri to raise up an heir to the inheritance.

* Assir — 1 Chron. 3:17

Matt. 1:12 — **Salathiel** — 1 Chron. 3:17, 19 & Luke 3:27

*Pedaiah — 1 Chron. 3:19

Matt. 1:13 — **Zerubbabel** — Luke 3:27

*7 sons of Zerubbabel — 1 Chron. 3:19, 20

Joseph's Legal Genealogy (likely skipping every other generation)..

Abiud to Joseph

Matthew 1:13-16

Matthew's focus as a tax collector is legal / inheritance.

Heli is likely Joseph and Mary's grandfather and they are cousins on Joseph's mother's side. (Gen. 24 & 29, Numbers 36)

Rhesa to Joseph

Luke 3:24-27

Luke's focus as a doctor is the bloodline.

---

* 1 Chronicles 3 Only - **Bold: Listed in Both Gospels**

Week Twenty-Six / Day Seven: The importance of evidence and prophecy

2 Peter 1:19-21, Luke 24:13-32

I can't help but empathise with the men in Luke 24:21 who said, "But we trusted that it had been he which should have redeemed Israel: and beside all this, today is the third day since these things were done. (Matt. 17:22-23) They were discouraged. They had believed, but then their faith was tested.

I can also see how critics could cast doubt about one thing or another, but their evidence is not proof against Scripture: sometimes we just do not have verifiable proof of specifics. But "Absence of evidence is not evidence of absence." Still, *we do* have evidence on our side.

The Creation model fits with science and the beginnings of life and intelligent life.
Manuscript evidence supports the Bible as a legitimate historical piece of literature and Alexander the Great shows the O.T. was written before Christ.
History gives credence to the existence of Jesus, Herod, James (the half brother of Jesus,) John the Baptist, Annas and Caiaphas, and Pontious Pilate
Archaeology gives evidence of King David and the flood.
Prophecy in its abundance between multiple writers and thousands of years being fulfilled by one man is a mathematical impossibility outside of a divine hand: especially since Jesus's birth was outside His control.

The weight of evidence is abundant. We can have faith in confidence that ours is not a blind faith, and we can live to please God knowing that His way is the best way.

Conclusion

Congratulations! You have covered so many topics in the past six months. Do you feel prepared to make that transition from relying on your parents as your spiritual guides to relying on Scripture and the Holy Spirit instead?

As I think of sending my own daughters out into the world someday, I would want nothing more than that exact transition. My heart's desire is for each of them and you to find God's word trustworthy and enough.

Yes, God's word is absolutely enough!

What a beautiful thought. I will leave you with that.

Have a great day and a wonderful next season of life.

Sincerely,
Melissa

Made in the USA
Monee, IL
22 February 2020

22147834R00115